# BY
# FAITH
# ALONE

## CONFESSIONS OF A
## BIBLE SMUGGLER

by
PATRICK KLEIN

"For several years I have been involved with Patrick's ministry and recently sent my son with him on a life-changing overseas trip. These stories are genuine, first-hand accounts of God's faithfulness to an ordinary man. Read them—and catch the vision!"

Kirk Cameron
TV and Film Actor/Producer

"I've been privileged to travel with Patrick and I've seen first-hand his heart to serve the King and to spread far and wide the Good News of a Savior Who loves us. I read through tears some of the amazing stories of God's faithfulness and protection, and of His overwhelming love that reaches into slums, into brothels and behind walls of oppression and hostility through the willing hands and feet of Patrick and his teams. Thank you, Patrick, for your willingness to go and serve, and for sharing these stories. Thank you, God, for showing Your power and grace in Patrick's life and ministry. My prayer is that every reader puts down this book with a new passion to GO! and reach the lost!"

Todd Nettleton, Director of Media and Public Relations
The Voice of the Martyrs—USA

"*By Faith Alone* is an appropriate title for Patrick Klein's new book. I've travelled with him on several occasions, and have witnessed his daily reliance on the Holy Spirit in serving people in need and ministering to the lost. When obstacles to gospel efforts seem insurmountable, Patrick and his team members pray and doors are opened. This book is a must read for anyone interested in learning more about Klein's amazing adventures and faith reliance in front-line ministry."

Gary Lane
International News Director/Senior Correspondent
CBN News

# BY
# FAITH
# ALONE

## CONFESSIONS OF A
## BIBLE SMUGGLER

by
PATRICK KLEIN

Published by:
Creative Press
P. O. Box 769000
Dallas, TX. 75376-9000

ISBN#978-0-89985-477-9

Special Note:
Names have been changed to protect the identities of those serving in closed nations.

*Thanks to all those who helped me in my walk with Jesus Christ through the years. Most of all, I would like to give all glory and honor to my Lord and Savior, Jesus Christ. I am forever grateful for Him rescuing me out of darkness and transferring me into His Kingdom of Light.*

# TABLE OF CONTENTS

# FOREWORD

I've traveled much of the world and met many kinds of people, but few have matched the dedicated life of Patrick Klein. The times I've been with him over the last 30 years have been inspiring and humbling.

'By Faith Alone' reveals what can happen when one person listens to the Holy Spirit on a moment-by-moment basis and simply follows. Patrick knows what Jesus meant when He said, "My sheep hear My voice."

This book contains miracle after miracle, happening all around one man and the friends who have been called alongside him—out of the spotlight, off the platform and away from the press. The stories will break your heart, move you to pray, and challenge you to listen and act.

The primary force in Patrick's character is well put in the old song, "I Have Decided To Follow Jesus." My prayer is that as you read these amazing true accounts, you will catch the same fire that has ignited Patrick's life. There's a hopeless, dying world out there, and God is calling for all to hear, "Whom shall I send, and who will go for us?"

—Don Francisco

# INTRODUCTION

"You did not choose Me, but I chose you and appointed you that you should go and bear fruit, and that your fruit should remain, that whatever you ask the Father in My name He may give you" (John 15:16 NKJV).

What causes someone to believe in something they have never seen? And can so radically change a person's life, they gratefully give all in order to share it with others? What impacts so powerfully, it propels a person to "go"—not only to those closest, but to the darkest, most forsaken places on earth—so others may know its life-giving message, too?

The answer is LOVE! There is no greater love than what God demonstrated when He was willing to sacrifice His own Son, Jesus, for our sins. Accepting this gift of salvation is an unforgettable experience and its power is undeniable. Once I felt the freedom His love brought—there was no turning back! It's the story of the Gospel that changed my life.

My journey began with a conflicted childhood and adolescence. I wrestled with fear and meaning in life, but it was in this tumultuous, dark place that God's light broke through and changed me forever. From that moment forward, my path was set to pursue Christ with the same intensity He had pursued me. My passion was to share His message of life so others could experience it, too!

In the beginning, I tried to do my best to minister the Gospel in my local city. God used some great experiences to help train me, and I received much counsel and love from those who did their part in preparing me to accept God's call when He said, "Go!"

Then I spent six months in Israel, where I gained a deeper understanding of those who suffer for their faith. Although it was a time of persecution, I learned that Jesus is my best friend and He will never leave or forsake me.

I realized this call to "Go" also meant I needed training, so I went to Bible School to deepen my knowledge of the Word and strengthen my relationship with the Lord. When I graduated, I was so excited—I thought, *I'm going to change the world, preach the Gospel, and see many people saved!*

However, God's plans, ways, and timing are sometimes different than ours. So, He sent me to the Philippines to work with a missionary family that was supported by my home church. The week after I arrived, they went to Hong Kong for nine weeks while I took care of things in their absence. It was intimidating being in an unfamiliar land, and within one week, the people I came to work with were gone. I was left by myself.

Instead of preaching the Gospel and changing the world, my job was to get the mail every day. This took 3-4 hours because I had to ride three different vehicles just to get to the post office, and then another three back home. It seemed so simple and mundane, but God asks us to be faithful wherever

He places us. We don't get to choose what we do, but we need to be faithful in all He calls us to.

However, that season came to an end and soon I was traveling. As an American, when I developed relationships with local Christians, it wasn't unusual to receive invitations to speak at churches, Bible studies, or Bible schools. I would get really excited and prepare a message, but every time I went to meet someone, there was a mix-up with the time or place and I wasn't able to preach. After this happened several times, I realized God was trying to get my attention.

I decided to fast and pray for eight days. I spent a lot of time on my face as God dealt with my prideful heart. I confessed, "Lord, I give up. I can't change the world. I can't do anything on my own. It's only You who can open the doors I need to walk through." I knew I had to let go. I said, "Lord, You're in charge of my life. I'm not in charge, You are. I surrender control of my life to You." I felt like he took my stony heart and replaced it with a heart that was clean, tender, and pliable in His hands. After repenting and crying out to Him during that fast, I felt my eyes were taken off of myself and put back on Him.

This season laid an important foundation for future ministry. Now, whenever I go to a country for the first time, I know I have to trust God to provide the contacts. Through many situations, I have learned that God's work is done by faith alone. I have to trust Him to see me through.

I later moved to China, where I'd planned to spend the rest

of my life. It was a faith-building time and I saw tremendous fruit, but it was not my final destination like I'd thought. I struggled with disappointment and feelings of failure when the door unexpectedly closed, but God opened up the world afterwards. For the next 25 years, I would have the honor of bringing God's Word and sharing the Gospel in many closed nations. It would be the fulfillment of words He spoke from the very beginning of this faith journey.

It was during my first Bible delivery trip into China that God revealed what He had called me to do. Twenty-seven years later, I still believe there's no greater gift than giving a person the Word of God in their language! Once you have experienced not only the lows that come with this kind of work, but the highs—the glorious outcome—where individuals are so overjoyed they cannot even speak, tears streaming down their faces out of gratitude from receiving God's holy, precious Word ... well, the decision to bring more ... doesn't even become an option any more. You are all the more motivated and compelled to follow the Lord's command to "Go!"

Truthfully, I feel honored to be a part of anything He has called me to do. I realize that many have gone before me, and I pray many more will still come ... even now! I am committed to following those who are willing to follow Christ, as the Apostle Paul claimed.

It is with complete humility that I share these testimonies. Yes, I was the man God chose for these particular events, but no man could have done any of this without Him. By faith, I have been able to follow His leading—and by faith, I continue gathering the courage it takes to keep serving where He leads.

The greater story, beneath the retelling of God's marvelous works, is this: He never abandons us. He will make a way where there is no way. He will open every door, so that His Name may be praised throughout all the Earth!

Come with me, as I share the history—times and places—where His mighty, everlasting power was at work, and every situation in the end revealed His glory.

20

# Chapter 1

# TREATED LIKE CRIMINALS

"It is right for me to feel this way about all of you, since I have you in my heart and, whether I am in chains or defending and confirming the gospel, all of you share in God's grace with me" (Philippians 1:7 NIV).

Several years ago, I had returned to Bangkok, Thailand after delivering Bibles to Vietnam. We began to pack Chinese Pastor Study Bibles for what we thought was going to be another routine trip of delivering Bibles to China. Now, I think to myself, *Is there ever just a 'routine trip' when you are going to a country whose government still wants to deny the Gospel?*

I don't remember the Lord cautioning us not to go, but I did sense we should have extra prayer coverage. I decided to call the intercessors in the U.S. and ask them to pray for our trip the next day. We also met a team of American intercessors at the guesthouse where we were staying who said they would pray for us.

Our team was up early the next morning. We had breakfast and finished packing the duffel bags full of Bibles. We wanted to get in as many as possible because we had learned that there were over a million Chinese pastors and church leaders who wanted and needed them. If they could possibly find them on the black market, they would pay six months to a year's salary to purchase one. It's estimated that for each of these Bibles distributed, at least 40 people will come to faith in Jesus Christ.

After we loaded the duffel bags into the van, a Burmese brother who was visiting us prayed for our trip. Then, our Thai brother who drove us to the airport, prayed over us. Between the intercessors who had committed to pray and these brother's fervent prayers, we had never had so much prayer covering us before we left for China—ever!

We checked in at the airport and were charged about $400.00 extra for the overweight luggage. Since we had delivered Bibles to Kunming for many years and only had problems one time with the hand wind tape players, I fully expected us to sail right through Customs unhindered. Our contacts in Kunming had been asking for these Bibles for over a year, so I was glad that we could help meet their need.

As I mentioned, that day seemed like any other day; it was just another trip to China to help our persecuted brothers and sisters by delivering Bibles to them. Yet, the Lord was preparing us for something very unusual and remarkable.

When we arrived in Kunming, I was surprised to see that security had been greatly increased. Every passenger was now required to put their bags through the X-ray machine. There were also more Customs guards at these points than I had ever seen before.

As I prayed, I sensed that Forrest (a 73 year-old grandfather) should go first, followed by his 15 year old grandson, Stephen. Normally, older people are respected and given more grace in Customs. This time, however, that was not the case. I could tell there was trouble when I saw Forrest and his grandson being pulled aside with their duffel bags. This meant only one thing … they were going to have their bags searched.

Then Steve and I were also pulled aside so they could search us. We could see that the Customs officials were visibly upset, as they proceeded to take us into their office. They made us remove all the Bibles from our bags. Then they took all my clothes out of my suitcase and began to search my personal bag. I also had a small, plastic bag in my hand that had personal papers, cash, and receipts in it.

The Customs officer demanded "Open the bag!"

I said, "These are my own personal belongings."

He replied, "You have no personal items in China. We can search anything we want at any time we want!"

After watching all of the Bibles being confiscated, I sensed the Holy Spirit speaking to me to stand up to the Customs officials—I didn't feel that He wanted me to just sign the receipt and go, as the normal process would be.

I gathered the team together to discuss what we should do. Our goal in bringing Bibles to China was to help the underground Church. Since we had been hearing so much propaganda about China and its religious freedom, we decided to stay in Customs until the Bibles were returned to us.

The Customs officers "refused" to return them to us—so we politely "refused" to leave. We prayed, "Father, we ask that You would be glorified in this situation and that the world would know the truth about the persecution of Christians in China and their need for Bibles."

I can tell you—the Chinese government is not used to having people stand up to them. They were confounded as to what to do with us. After about an hour, they asked us again to leave their office. However, this time they agreed to move us to the lounge across the large Customs room where there were couches and a television. I think they fully expected us to back down and leave, but we felt to stay the course.

Before the trip, our Chinese contacts had continued to cry out for Bibles, explaining they could not get copies of the Word of God. The media in China was circulating a different story, claiming the government was printing millions of Bibles and leaving the impression there was surplus to meet the demand.

Even much of the media in the United States portrays a view that is contrary to what we have experienced firsthand. They report that Bibles are readily available and there is freedom of religion in China.

I even heard on a Christian radio station in America about a woman from China's state-sanctioned Three Self Church. She was addressing a group of Evangelical Church leaders in Texas and stated emphatically: "There is no persecution of Christians in China, there are no pastors in prison for their faith; you are free to believe whatever you want in China, and please, don't bring us anymore Bibles. We have enough Bibles!"

She implied the Chinese Church did not need help from the Church in the West. This is contrary to what our contacts report in China. I would rather believe a Chinese pastor who has spent more than 20 years in prison for his faith than a deceived government puppet, who tells a compromised Church what they want to believe.

With approximately 100 million Christians in China,[1] and the Church growing by an estimated 10,000 new believers a day,[2] the millions of Bibles printed by the only state-permitted press in the last 25 years have not been enough to meet the needs of existing believers, let alone provide for new converts. And not surprisingly, a large percentage of these Bibles are exported for foreign business purposes. Of the Bibles that remain in China, distribution is controlled and monitored, leaving rural house churches without direct access.[3]

Believers are willing to risk everything to obtain God's Word. They are unashamed of the Gospel and the power of God for the salvation of all who believe (Romans 1:16). They are willing to lay down their lives, so they can share Christ with others. They encourage us to do the same.

With all these thoughts running through our minds, we quickly prayed and continued to stand firm to get the Bibles where they were needed. We decided we would either get Bibles to our brothers and sisters or expose the hypocrisy of a government who claimed they had religious freedom, but still would not let Bibles into their country.

As a team, we decided to fast and pray. We only drank water for the first 20 hours, while we waited in Customs. Our sleep was often interrupted, as the Customs officers kept waking us up—telling us that we needed to leave the airport.

They informed us, "You must apply to the Religious Affairs Office to petition them to get your Bibles back." We knew this was only a game the Chinese government plays to try to appease foreigners. When I asked where their office was, they said, "Somewhere in the Yunnan Province. Go to a hotel and check the Internet." However, we knew their plan was to just get us to leave the Customs hall. Once we had left, they could say it was not their problem.

We repeatedly asked the officials to show us a copy of the law. It took them almost 20 hours to show us a copy, and then it was written in Mandarin. This law was approved on June 1,

2007, and it stated that any foreigner coming to China is only allowed to bring in one piece of religious material for their own personal use. If a foreigner brings more than one piece, it must be pre-approved by the Religious Affairs Office. Of course, they would never approve Bibles to be carried into their country.

Before leaving on the trip, I had decided to add International Calling service to my cell phone. The Lord used this so that we could make phone calls from the Customs hall. We called the White House, but only got the switchboard operator since it was the weekend. We tried Senator John McCain's voicemail, but it was full. Then I called Bob Fu with China Aid Ministry. He told us that we could sign the receipt and pick up the Bibles on the way back out of the country. I knew the Lord had said to take a stand, so Bob said he would send out a press release. He did, and included my cell phone number on it.

The Associated Press picked up the story and sent it all over the world. A lady from the AP called me to verify the story. She asked if she could call me every couple of hours to make sure we were alright. She said that if they tried to physically remove us from Customs to call the AP immediately, and they would have someone at the airport within 15 minutes. She said that even if the U.S. Government wouldn't help us, the AP would!

Our intention was not to cause trouble, but rather to help the Chinese Christians, like we had been doing for over 20 years. We prayed that God would somehow use the situation to bring glory to His Name, and that the truth about religious persecution of Christians would be brought out to the world.

We were amazed at how He used it to cause a stir throughout the world. We received phone calls from all over the U.S., the U.K., New Zealand, Colombia, the major news networks, newspapers, and radio stations worldwide. We never expected it would be called an "international event."

Almost everyone was supportive, and we were able to tell them why we were in China, and why we refused to leave the Customs area. We shared that our ordeal was minimal compared to what many of our brothers and sisters in China face every day because of their faith in Jesus Christ.

In January, 2007, *The Voice of the Martyrs* printed this information:

"The human rights record in China is one of the worst in the world. Its system of 're-education through labor' detains hundreds of thousands each year in work camps, without even a court hearing. Again, in 2007, church property and Bibles were confiscated. Christians were harassed, questioned, arrested and imprisoned. More Christians are in prison or under detention in China than any other country.

The House-Church-Movement, which is the unregistered churches and comprises of approximately 90 percent of China's

Christians, endures unimaginable persecution; yet, it stands on its commitment to preach the Gospel, no matter the cost ... Christians in prison are routinely beaten and abused."

The U.S. Embassy staff in Beijing was unaware of this new law in China and offered to come to our aid. They called the Customs office and requested to see the law that Customs claimed we had broken. After interpreting the law into English, they told us that, in fact, we had broken the law of China. The decision came down that the Customs officials were not going to return our Bibles to us while we were in China, but we could get them back when we left the country.

After 26 hours of intermittent sleep due to repeated interruptions of the Customs officials yelling at us, tired and battle weary—the team decided to go to a hotel and get a decent meal, a hot shower, and some sleep. The phone continued to ring for the next several days, as we did more interviews with people from all over the world. It was reassuring to see that people wanted to know what was really happening in China.

Naturally, now that we were considered to be trouble-makers, the government had spies assigned to follow us around. So for the next two days, we acted like we were just tourists. I actually caught a man coming out of our hotel room. He'd been in there to search through the belongings in our room. You can imagine how surprised he was to run into me face-to-face.

A Chinese lady, posing as a reporter from a Christian radio station in Hong Kong, called us twice. She kept asking us leading questions, trying to discover who our contacts were in China and their addresses and phone numbers. Needless to say, she didn't receive any information from us.

There were also five young men staying just down the hall from us. They happened to be electronically equipped with laptop computers and cell phones. When we returned to the airport, three hours early, the Customs officials were already waiting for us.

There were ten Customs officials at the airport; they had two video cameras and one still camera. However, when we took out one of our cameras, they threatened to take it away.

They did give us back the Bibles, but we were watched constantly, and then escorted to Immigration by Security. This was another preventative move on their part, so that we couldn't turn back. We felt like we were being deported. We were treated like criminals—just for carrying Bibles to a country that claims to have religious freedom.

I realize now, that even though we didn't get to take the Bibles in, the world heard the truth about what is happening in China. Since our trip, we have heard reports that many people were praying for us, but more importantly, they are now aware of the Chinese Christians' plight and are praying for them.

Sometimes I hear people say, 'It's not my problem. Why should I care if they don't get a Bible in China?' But I believe if we really have the heart of God and love the Word of God, we'll want everyone around the world who wants it to have it. If God's people don't care, who's going to care?

A few years ago, we were challenged when we heard about a house church in China that had one hand-copied New Testament for over 100 believers. Can you imagine having to share your Bible with 100 people? I think we would value God's Word more if we had to share it with others. What if I only had access to the Bible for one hour a week, would I be reading it, or maybe hand copying the precious text? If I could only have one page of scripture, which one would I choose?

To have God's Word in my language is truly a gift and I need to treasure it! While most Americans have multiple Bibles in their homes, many of our brothers and sisters around the world do not have a single copy of God's Word in their language. We have been given much in America, but Jesus said to whom much is given, much is required (Luke 12:48). We have a responsibility to meet the needs of those around us. We need to make sure the Word of God gets into our brothers and sisters hands.

The needs of the Chinese Church can seem insurmountable. Yet our faith and confidence is in an awesome God who can multiply what is carried across borders! My continual prayer is for the Church from all parts of the world to *hear* the call, *go* to prayer, and act on behalf of our persecuted family!

# Chapter 2

# TRIALS AND TRIBULATION

"You will have tribulation for ten days. Be faithful until
death, and I will give you the crown of life"
(Revelation 2:10b NASB).

In the fall of 1992, God gave me a promise. And it wasn't
just any promise. I was about to leave for Afghanistan for
the first time with a good friend on a mission to take Bibles
to the Muslim people there. As I waited for the boarding
announcement, I sat with my Bible on my lap, praying about

the trip. That's when the words of Revelation 2:10 jumped out at me from the pages of Scripture. "You will have tribulations for ten days." Though written for another time and place, I could sense that these words were also a promise for me.

Now the airlines began to make my boarding announcement. I tucked the verse away to ponder on later and we boarded the plane. Mark and I had worked together in Hong Kong, taking Bibles to persecuted Christians in China. Both of us had prayed for God to take us where the need for His Word was the greatest. Right then, we felt compelled to bring Bibles to the people in Afghanistan.

Afghanistan had been a country in conflict for decades, and in 1992, it was shaping up to be an especially bad year of civil conflict. At the time of our trip, Iran-backed extremist Gulbuddin Hekmatyar was fighting Burhanuddin Rabbani, a moderate Muslim and the leader of the country, along with the Tajik leader, Ahmad Massoud. Rabbani and Massoud were in control of the government. Hekmatyar wanted to make Afghanistan more like Iran, which was strictly Islamic—oppressing women and restricting any influence from the West. Innocent people were getting caught in the middle, which is what usually happens.

As Mark and I flew into Kabul, we looked down on a city that was cradled by mountains, with a brilliantly blue sky above and a rolling carpet of arid land below. In the west was a backdrop of the snow-covered Paghman Mountains, which showcased the beauty of this ancient city. From the air, it was hard to imagine modern artillery being used in such a remote and timeless place.

Then we landed. Primitive and poor, the airport had previously been hit by rockets; it was in bad shape. Our suitcases laden with scriptures were brought to us on a flatbed trailer, which was pulled behind a slow-moving farm tractor. Inside the terminal, the bathroom was partially bombed out, leaving us to wonder not only what violence had taken place there, but how recently it had happened.

The first time you arrive in a new country, there is always the shock of the unfamiliar, the foreign. For me, it was the weaponry on display that stood out the most. Though I was raised in Wyoming, where a truck is not complete without a gun rack, it was still alarming to see men with bazookas, AK-47s, and other firepower—all within easy reach. Adding to this starkly hostile setting were the ever-present tanks, sitting at strategic corners or patrolling the streets.

We did not waste any time at the airport. We quickly hailed a cab at the curb. As our taxi driver made his way through the city streets toward our hotel, we caught a glimpse of daily life. Women, covered from head to toe in their full-length chadors, walked purposefully to and from the markets. Only a small mesh opening allowed them to see where they were walking. Occasionally, we would see a woman raise the screen so she could see better or perhaps breathe more freely. Many had small children in tow, beautiful with their large, wise eyes and shy smiles.

Mark and I checked into a modest hotel and settled in for a week's stay. That night, we could look out from the balcony and see the fireworks. I don't mean 4th of July fireworks, but gunfire that lit up the sky far outside the city. We could hear the distant rockets hiss and then explode as they hit their targets. The civil war was happening right in front of us, but far enough outside of Kabul that it did not seem to impact the city itself. We listened to the popping sound of explosions as they punctuated the still night air. How could we not pray for the people of Afghanistan!

Coming from the baggage claim earlier, we had walked right through Customs without any incident. This was rare since we had 110 booklets, which contained the Gospels of Luke and Mark, all of them written in the native Dari language. They do not like Gospel literature to say the least, and if they find it, they will often either hold you for questioning or confiscate it. We knew God had already gone before us.

The next morning, Mark and I asked the Lord for direction in how and where He wanted us to distribute the literature. We decided to begin by just walking through the city. We wanted to wait on the Lord to direct us in giving away the Gospel portions as we went.

Among the many we met that day was a shopkeeper, who gave us a long, curious look before accepting the booklet. "Is this Christian?" he asked. Mark said it was, and the man asked for more to give to his family members and friends. Like many of the people we encountered, he was very open to the Gospel.

As Americans, we really stood out in the crowds. Besides me and Mark, there was only one other foreigner in the country at the time—a French man we had met one day on the street who was looking for drugs. He wore a bright red coat and a French beret. He didn't seem to mind that he was a willing target for snipers. But I believe God used our foreignness as a way to spark the Afghan people's curiosity and open doors for conversation.

Another day, while we were out walking, we met two young doctors who wanted to know why we were in Kabul. We invited the doctors to our hotel room to talk. One of them also brought his brother. After visiting a while, we showed them the "JESUS" video in their Dari dialect. Because an early curfew was in effect, they quickly left after the video, but the doctors returned the next day and asked us many questions.

Six years before, one of them had received a New Testament from a British missionary. Both men were very receptive to the Gospel and we prayed with them to be able to come to a full understanding of who Jesus is.

That week we also visited the old American Embassy. At that time, it had been shut down for three years. There, we listened to two Afghans who had worked for the embassy. They shared their frustrations with us. Both seemed to be broken-hearted that their country had been through so much warfare. They spoke of how those with guns would steal from those with smaller guns or from those with no guns at all. We could only listen and share with them the hope that comes from knowing Jesus. Afterwards, they let us pray for them and their country.

Having explored Kabul a bit, our next destination was a place called Mazar-e-Sharif, which is known for its stunning blue-tiled mosque. It is the second-largest city in Afghanistan, and some call this the "capital of the North."

We rolled in on a dusty bus, after passing through some incredibly rugged and bombed-out country. At one point, we had to leave our bus to walk through a landslide, which had been caused by a heavy rainstorm. It was now blocking the road. Boulders, the size of cars, had rolled down the canyon, and mud had wiped out entire villages. It was no wonder there were these road blocks. We slogged through the mud for about a mile and then boarded another bus which was waiting to take us on to Mazar-e-Sharif.

Our plans were to cross over to Termez and then on to Tajikistan, Kazakhstan, and Kirghizstan. We spent two days in Mazar-e-Sharif, and then traveled about 45 minutes by taxi to the border. There we met a young, helpful soldier who spoke English very well. He said that we would need an exit permit to leave the country of Afghanistan. We had not known this, and now it would take a trip back to Mazar-e-Sharif to get the necessary stamp.

"Let me talk to my army colonel and see what I can do," the young man offered. He really liked Americans and I thanked God for giving us time with him. After about twenty minutes, he came back with permission to let us leave the country. Again, this was nothing less than Divine intervention.

Now that we could leave, we had to find a ride across the bridge that separated us from Tajikistan. Pedestrians were not allowed to cross, so we waited alongside a Pakistani man who was also hoping to get across.

Suddenly, a Jeep that was carrying two drunken Russians careened toward us, stopping suddenly in a cloud of dust. Loudly, and in broken English, they offered us a ride. With no better options to choose from, the three of us climbed into the back. The men asked us where we were from, and I told them Mark and I were Americans.

"No way! You can't be from America!" shouted the Russian in the driver's seat.

"Yes," I replied, "We are from America." *Maybe we should have waited for another ride*, I thought.

"No," the man repeated, "You can't be from America— we love Americans!" After we showed them our passports, they were ecstatic. "Wow! We love you! We love America!" Again, a Divine set-up!

The ride was quickly over and they dropped us off at the border. The funny part is, they were quite impressed with themselves for having met and helped two Americans. We were feeling pretty good, too, that is until the police at the border told us: "You can't come through here—you're Americans. Only Russians and Afghans are allowed to pass this way."

When we protested, they picked up the phone and called their KGB officials, who confirmed: "No, you are not allowed to enter Tajikistan."

By then, the war had really broken out in Kabul, which I reminded the officer. Thousands of refugees were streaming from Kabul, trying to stay ahead of the fighting that had moved into the city.

"We can't go back there!" I told him.

"Well," he said, shrugging, "That's your problem. Go to Iran."

Unlike our friendly Russian chauffeurs, the Iranians were feeling very anti-American right then. When I said that I really did not want to go to Iran, the officer suggested that we fly out of the country and head somewhere else. Unfortunately, most of the planes were being used for target practice, making this a less-than-appealing way to leave the country.

Reluctantly, we decided to return to Kabul by bus. During that long ride back, we passed people who were riding in donkey carts, on the backs of dump trucks, in buses, hanging off the tops and sides of buses—grasping at any means of transportation to escape the barrage of rockets and gunfire.

Finally, back in Kabul, we got off the bus and flagged a taxi. Mark had a visa to get into Pakistan, which was our next choice of destinations. Having planned to go to Tajikistan, I did not have a visa for Pakistan. So our first destination was the Pakistan Embassy to apply for my visa. On the way there, a rocket sailed over the top of our taxi. Our driver ducked low, muttering, "Oooh, bad, very bad." The nearness of the fighting was startling.

At the Pakistan Embassy we hurried to the entrance, hoping to get my tourist visa approved quickly. Two uniformed guards stopped us at the door. "Sorry, we are closed," one of them said. "Come back tomorrow."

"What do you mean, 'You're closed?'" I asked. "You can't be closed. We want to go to Pakistan tonight because the war is heating up." I was starting to wonder what we would do if we could not get out of Kabul soon.

Unmoved, the guard, who seemed to be in charge repeated, "Sorry, we're closed. Come back tomorrow. We're open tomorrow from eight to four."

"I can't come back tomorrow. There's a war going on."

"We're closed," he insisted. "Come back tomorrow."

"If I come back tomorrow, how long will it take to get a Pakistan tourist visa?"

"Five working days!" he stated. The expression on his face never changed.

"What?!" I was nearly shouting now. I repeated, "Five working days? You guys aren't that busy, and I'm an American. We've done a lot to help your country!"

"Five working days," he repeated. "Come back tomorrow."

Seeing that we weren't going to get anywhere with him, we left. Mark and I decided we would try to go out the other border, through Jalalabad into Pakistan, hoping they would let me in without a visa.

We flagged down a taxi and got in. As we were riding along, a military vehicle signaled our driver to pull over to the side of the road. Two stern and angry-looking soldiers ordered us out of the vehicle. We were annoyed when they began searching through our bags, but our annoyance turned to fear when they demanded that our driver turn over the keys to the taxi.

Immediately, the driver began to shout at us, "GET BACK INTO THE TAXI!" Mark and I quickly ducked around the soldiers and scrambled into the car as he sped off. At that point, we had no idea what was happening. The driver began to explain to us, "They had guns! They were going to try to steal my taxi."

We had been told at the American Embassy that the country was in a state of anarchy, and here was the evidence. We prayed right there for those soldiers and for the whole country, which seemed to be disintegrating all around us.

After taking us as far as he was willing to go, the driver left us to wait by the roadside for another means of transportation. It was still a 12-hour drive to the Pakistan border. After a long wait, a van stopped and we were able to hire the driver to take us there. We were now traveling the same direction as the refugees; all of us were trying to get out of the country any way possible.

We had not gone far before a soldier pulled us over. Mark and I exchanged a look, expecting to be ordered out of the car for another time. The soldier just looked inside at us, and said, "You go any farther, and they will kill you." I was starting to realize that Pakistan was not going to be our destination. Whether or not we both had visas wasn't even going to be the issue.

"If you take this van down the road any further," he continued, "the radicals are going to blow it up and kill you two Americans." We opted to turn around and go back into the war zone. Again, we had to push our way past the fleeing masses.

Earlier, Mark and I had made friends with some guys from Rabbani's government forces. We looked them up when we returned to the city. Thankfully, these friends let us stay that night at their army base along the highway.

During the middle of the night, we were repeatedly awakened by volleys of gunfire. I cautiously looked out the windows and saw soldiers shooting their guns up in the air. I could hear them clapping and rejoicing, "The war is over! It is finished! It's done!"

Mark and I were elated to hear such good news. We went back to sleep, finally feeling hopeful. But the next day, the rockets started coming again and we knew it was not over. We spent two nights at the army base, and then we were told it was not even safe for us to stay there any longer.

Some of our new friends took us to a bombed-out shelter. We were surprised to learn that it had once been a country club. Not long before, it had been a hideout for the generals to use while making their strategic plans for the war. It was an eerie place, but we decided to go in and take a look around because we were in such great need of a place to stay.

The lobby of this former country club was still quite nice, even though most of the building had been destroyed. We found a small group of about a dozen men dressed in military uniforms who were sitting around on couches. I decided to start a conversation with a friendly young man wearing army fatigues who was casually holding a submachine gun in his hand.

"I'm a Christian," I said, "How about you—what are you?"

"I'm a Muslim. I believe in Islam," he answered.

"Really?" I asked.

"Yes," he replied, frowning. "You, come with me."

Not sure what to expect, I followed him into a side room that was not far away. I started to feel a little nervous when he locked the door from the inside. Then he did something totally unexpected. He laid his gun down on a ping-pong table and told me he was a bodyguard for one of the generals. Suddenly he exploded, "I hate this gun! I hate this war, and I hate the Koran!" He continued, "Jesus and the Bible—that's the truth."

I was surprised, but sensing God at work, I continued to talk to this young man. I learned that he had heard the Gospel when he had been trained as a soldier in Russia, but had not yet given his life to Christ. I shared more of the Gospel with my new friend, and later, Mark and I prayed with him for his salvation. We were certain this was a divine appointment that the Lord had set up for us. He was very receptive, and we could see an immediate change in him.

Although he had been friendly to us before, now he was eager to help us. After we prayed, he took us to an apartment that was close by, and we stayed there for the night. We shared more of the faith with him, and he was very receptive to the things of the Lord. We were so grateful to have a place to stay, even though the apartment next door had been bombed and there was a huge, gaping hole in the wall. All the doors and windows had been blown out, and it seemed less than secure.

The next day, our friend said he would take us to a hotel where it would be safer for us. He first took us to the Inter-Continental Hotel, but the cost was a $100.00 a night. This was not only considerably more than we could afford, but at the time it had no water or electricity, and the restaurant's menu consisted of only one item—potatoes.

We declined to stay and went back to the Hotel Spinzar. This hotel was a large, five-story building in the center of town where we had originally been. It was just the basics, but at least it was affordable and still had running water. Our hotel room at the Spinzar looked out over the Kabul River and we could see a marketplace along the river.

By this time, we had been denied entrance at the border of Tajikistan, threatened on the road to Pakistan, and forced to return to the war zone of Kabul. Pakistan still seemed the best option, so on the third day back in Kabul, I decided to apply for a Pakistani visa and leave my passport at their embassy for the required five-day wait. When the fifth day had finally elapsed, I walked to the embassy to pick up my documents while Mark stayed at the hotel.

As I stepped out of the hotel and began to walk down the street, I saw people looking up at the sky. Following the direction of their gaze, I saw six puffs of smoke hanging in the air. The next thing I knew, everyone had scattered for shelter. I ran to hide behind a low stone wall, crouching down as far as possible.

Soon explosions began to rock the ground, six in quick succession. The air filled with smoke and debris, and I could hear the rending of metal close by. Screams and wails from men and women echoed all around me. I waited about a minute for the air to clear before peeking out. Then I stood up from my low position behind the wall. I looked around and gaped at the destruction on the street. About forty feet away was a taxi with a hole in the roof and both doors blown open. Two men lay dead, half dangling from the taxi. All around that area, people were struggling from behind their hiding places and staggering into the street.

Looking for a safer place, in case more rockets were fired, I ran into a government building next door. As I got there, wounded people were being brought into the building by those who could still walk. One woman being helped inside had blood running down her head from several injuries to her face. A man walked in with his pants drenched in blood. Both the dead and wounded were scattered everywhere. My plans to retrieve my passport were abandoned, and I turned back to the hotel. As I entered the hotel lobby, the men at the counter warned me not to go out. I told them, "It's too late now," and climbed the stairs to our room.

At the time, Gulbuddin Hekmatyar was using something like siege warfare. He would wait until the people ran out of food, usually about three days, and then bomb the markets when the people started to venture out for food. This had been one of those attacks and since our hotel was so close to the market, it was also hit.

I walked into the room, relieved to see that Mark was still there and unharmed. We went out onto the little balcony off of our room to get a better look at the destruction. While I had been down in the street, a rocket had exploded in front of our hotel. Mark, who had been packing his suitcase, heard the sound and quickly moved into the entry way. Just seconds later, two pieces of shrapnel lodged into the wall where he had been standing. They would have been in the back of his head. His quick move had no doubt saved his life.

As I walked through the room to check for other damage, I found pieces of concrete that had fallen onto my bed. Venturing back out onto our balcony, we could see bodies everywhere, broken and bleeding. One elderly man across the street had been hit by shrapnel and lay dead in a pool of blood. His son stood over him, wailing loudly with grief, his hands up in the air as he paced back and forth. People loaded the injured into taxis for transport to the hospital. The dead were put into the trunks of cars.

After our near brush with death on the balcony, Mark and I were determined to leave the Spinzar Hotel. Earlier, we had met a lady who worked for the BBC. She told us she was not living in her house and that we could stay there. We decided to take her up on the offer. It was not luxurious, but it felt safer than that bombed-out hotel.

We made our way to the Pakistan Embassy. All along the way there were pools of blood where people had been wounded or killed. There was so much hopelessness and despair. I saw one lady who had a baby in her arms. She only had a small blanket to cover him. She was talking to one of the soldiers, obviously in great distress. Her husband and all her other children were killed—her extended family were all dead. Her home was demolished, and all she had was her baby in its small blanket. She was sobbing hysterically. The men just laughed and mocked her; they showed no concern for her plight. As I watched, I sensed God's love for this woman who had lost so much and prayed that Jesus would reveal Himself to her.

One night, Mark went to find food for us. I stayed "home" because I was still feeling sick. I had a bout of malaria for five days while we were staying at the Spinzar Hotel. Suddenly, more rockets came shrieking in. I could hear them part the air as they flew over. Again, people on the streets ran for cover. The shrapnel from these rockets could penetrate almost anything, and the destruction was just as devastating as all the others we had already witnessed.

Still on the street, Mark was called into a nearby home right after a rocket exploded close by. A picture window in the house had blown out. The family who was living there took him down into the basement and fed him some dinner.

Meanwhile, I was back at the BBC reporter's house, not knowing where Mark was and getting very nervous because he had now been gone for several hours. I was truly afraid that Mark was lying dead in the streets of Kabul. When he finally arrived a few hours later, he told me of the new friends he had made and the destruction that was stalking the streets.

The next day, while out trying to find a way for us to leave the country, I heard a rocket whizzing into the area of the city I was in. It did not hit the street where I was standing this time, but it was still close. This was the eighth day since we had returned to Kabul.

I knew I was weary and needed to go to God in prayer. I broke down and started to cry. I wept, "God, I just can't handle this any more. I can't stand this!"

At that moment, I felt the Lord speak to my heart, "Didn't I tell you ten days? Had I taken you out on the first day, you would not have known what war is. Now that you have lived in war, you have experienced it firsthand. You can understand, and you can empathize with people in their war-torn countries. Didn't I tell you ten days that you would have tribulation, but if you overcame it, you would see the crown of life?" The words from Revelation came rushing back to my mind as I continued to weep before the Lord; my tears turned to those of brokenness and gratitude.

The next day, I continued to try and find somebody who could help us get out, but there was no one leaving in any direction. Then, by God's providence, I met some people who talked to the Minister of Electricity and Water. He said he would let us go out in his entourage, which was heading for the Pakistan border. Thank God! By this time, I had been able to get my passport back from the Pakistan Embassy, and I finally had my tourist visa.

We left Kabul the next day at 8:00 am (the 10th day) in a bus with about thirty other people. Three Toyota pickups filled with soldiers carrying bazookas and submachine guns accompanied us. Two trucks were in front of us and one came along behind. The minister rode in the second Toyota pickup. It took about 12 hours, and at one point, the minister and his soldiers stopped at a village for dinner.

Meanwhile, our entourage continued toward the Pakistan border. The soldiers in control of that area stopped us about an hour later. They refused to let us go any further. Thirty minutes later, the minister arrived in his pickup truck. After he talked to the men, they quickly let us pass.

When we got to the Pakistani border around 10:30 that night, the gate across the road was closed and locked. The head border guard came and welcomed the minister, Mark, and me with a cup of tea. We sat down at a table while they took our passports and stamped us into the country; we were free to go. They opened the gate, and we finally made it into Pakistan.

The minister continued to take good care of us. He had his men escort us to a hotel, check us in, and make sure we were safe. I could hardly believe we had made it out of Afghanistan in one piece! Mark hurried to phone his parents back in Houston to let them know he was alive and well. When he got them on the phone, he told them we were both fine and had made it safely out of Afghanistan.

"Really? What's going on in Afghanistan?" his parents asked.

Mark could not believe it. Almost shouting, he cried, "THERE'S A WAR GOING ON! We've been stuck in a war zone for ten days. There were fifteen hundred rockets dropped on Kabul and about a thousand people killed in the last ten days."

"Well, we haven't heard anything about that. All we hear about on the news is the election." Incredibly, they had heard nothing of the war in Afghanistan. I learned that day how insulated Americans can be from the realities of life in other countries.

God really gave me a love for the Afghan people during that trip. I have been back to Afghanistan once since then to take in more Gospel literature. I am excited to see what God is doing in Afghanistan. The people there have lived through the Mujahedeen, the Russian occupation, the Taliban, and the U.S. war. They do not want to be Communist and many do not want to be Islamic. People are asking, "What is the truth?" They are searching. I believe we have an opportunity now to bring the Gospel to them like never before.

After it was all over, I thanked God I had been able to endure the ten days. Of course, the Lord was a shield for both Mark and me. We had overcome by God's grace, and we were certainly looking forward to the promise of receiving the crown of life.

# Chapter 3

## BEGINNING THE JOURNEY

"Whosoever therefore shall confess Me before men, him will I confess also before my Father which is in heaven" (Matthew 10:32 KJV).

I feel I've gotten somewhat ahead of my story. Some of you might be wondering, "How did an ordinary guy like me end up in a place like Afghanistan?" The truth is that it was not a simple journey. God had a lot of patience with me and guided my steps through a painful childhood. My search for meaning through my adolescent years is what finally led me to a relationship with Him that radically changed my life.

The journey began when I was born in Greendale, Wisconsin, on May 22, 1962, the fourth child of what would be a family of five children. There were four of us boys and we had one older sister. My childhood was not a happy time. I felt like I could not make my mother happy, that I was unloved and unwanted. My parents divorced when I was eight years old. This was an especially difficult time for me because I wasn't close to my mother and my dad worked long hours as a self-employed plumber. After the divorce, we were taken out of the Catholic school we had been attending in Milwaukee and put into a public school across the street.

This was during the early 1970's, when divorce was still relatively uncommon. There were only two families in my new school that had experienced divorce, and I was embarrassed as our family fell apart. The combination of my mother's rejection, my father's emotional distance, and the sense of being a social outcast at school, all led me to withdraw into myself more and more.

In school, people called me "Smiley" because I would always put a smile on my face. What they could not see was that I was dying on the inside. I was hurting, lonely and empty. Several times I contemplated suicide, thinking I would not be missed if I died. I am thankful that the Lord had His hand on me even then and did not allow me to take my own life.

My dad remarried a year after the divorce, and shortly after that we moved from Wisconsin to Wyoming. In high school, I rebelled against my parents and partied for a short time. I drank with friends and even experimented with drugs a few times, but these things only increased the emptiness I felt inside.

In 1980, I graduated from high school. A few months later I travelled to Nevada to see my mother for the first time in ten years. It was very difficult for me; so many years of separation had done some damage.

During this time, the Iran hostage crisis occurred and I had to register for the draft. At eighteen years of age, I was scared to death at the thought of ending up in Iran with a bullet in my head. The profound sense of meaninglessness that plagued my earlier years had persisted into my late teens. Now with the added weight of this fear and confusion, it was a lot to bear.

Though our family had faithfully attended church every week, for me, the Bible was just a lot of words on a page. I remember reading about the Apostle Paul in Sunday school and wondering why we studied him and his trips.

Then on September 8, 1980, my whole life was transformed. That night, I met Jesus Christ. I had seen a poster advertising a Don Francisco concert in Glenrock, Wyoming, which was a small town about twenty miles from my home. Don is an award-winning recording artist and one of the pioneers of contemporary Christian music.

I did not know it at the time, but Don is known for putting God's love and grace into song, explaining the Bible in ways that everyone can understand. When I saw that poster, I was inexplicably drawn to it. I felt that I needed to attend the concert. Even though I was not sure why, I just knew I had to be there.

Three of my friends decided to go with me the night of the concert. After we arrived, we stood in the doorway for a while because the room was so packed. After a while, people moved in closer and we found a place to sit. There was an incredible sense of peace in that place, and I felt pulled toward God by the songs. My defenses melted away as I listened to the beautiful music. I saw two other high school acquaintances, who I had heard were involved in drugs, but both of them had light streaming from their faces and their hands were raised in worship to God.

Don sang many songs that night. I could feel the presence of God. He then sang a song called, "Give Your Heart a Home." It talked about smiling faces that hid empty and confused hearts. It was as though my whole life was being exposed in those few minutes and I was laid bare before God and all the people. I got really angry. Someone must have written to Mr. Francisco to tell him about my life and he must have written a song about me, exposing my deception in front of all these people!

I felt embarrassed and ashamed because the mask had come off. Then God spoke to my heart and said, "Don doesn't know you, but I know you; I'm the One you have been searching for all this time. I'm the One who died for you; I'm Jesus!"

I had felt doomed to hell with no way out, developing strange beliefs that were not scriptural. But, fighting against my fear, at the end of the concert I went to the front of the church and asked Don to pray for me. I repented of my sins and was born again by the Holy Spirit that night. Now, there was peace in my heart and a joy that was indescribable.

Later, as I lay on my bed that night, I just laughed from deep down in my heart. I finally knew, without any doubt, my sins had been forgiven and I now had a new life—a future.

I knew something happened in my heart that night, but I had no idea how it would change the course of my life. On the way back home to Casper, my friends mocked both me and Don, making fun of those "Jesus freaks." But I had changed; I was no longer the man I used to be. I soon realized, however, that not everyone would want what I had.

I was so excited about my new faith in Jesus. I wanted to share this truth with all my family and friends. The next night, I hugged my dad for the first time in years and I told him that I loved him. He had tears in his eyes. I witnessed to him and his wife, and told them they would go to hell if they did not repent. As you can imagine, this was not received well. I was zealous, but I did not know how to use tact or wisdom.

I suddenly found I had an intense hunger for the Word of God and began to read the Bible as I never had before. My Bible had always just sat on the bookshelf, but now, this Book was alive and I could not get enough of it. I sought out a pastor who could help me grow in my relationship with the Lord. I quickly joined a Baptist Church in town, even though I had been raised first in the Catholic Church and then attended a Lutheran Church after my dad remarried.

The minister at my dad's church believed everybody was saved, regardless of what they believed. But as I studied the Word of God, I realized that Jesus is the only way. This minister also denied the Virgin Birth and did not believe the Bible was the Word of God. He believed that all religions contained parts of the truth and that all together they comprised the truth.

At one point, he told me that I was just going through a "phase," that I would "come to my senses," and come back to the denomination of the church he pastored. I defended myself by explaining to him that I was now a Baptist, and John the Baptist in the New Testament was also a Baptist, and since the Baptists were an older denomination than his, they must be right. I was excited about my new faith, but I still lacked knowledge.

Of course, I know better now and realize that God has saved people in many churches and from many denominations. I also know that John was not a Baptist, as in a particular religion, but rather he baptized repentant people. I was learning, but I still had much to learn.

I was quite shy, self-conscious, and insecure because of my up-bringing. Getting saved doesn't automatically change your personality. But God began to work in my life to build my confidence in Him. About eight months after I was saved, a friend took me to a Christian coffeehouse called The Sycamore Tree. It was there that I met some friends who mentored me in my walk with the Lord and I was baptized in the Holy Spirit.

My friend, Mike, offered to take me out on the streets that night to witness in front of the Wonder Bar in downtown Casper. I was excited, but I was also very afraid of talking to strangers about receiving salvation through Jesus Christ.

Late that night, Mike and I were standing in front of the Wonder Bar. My stomach was in knots. Mike saw my nervousness and shared the Scripture with me, "Whosoever therefore shall confess Me before men, him will I confess also before my Father which is in heaven" (Matthew 10:32). Right then and there, God touched me and gave me the boldness I needed to share the Gospel with people.

Mike and Marilyn, the leaders of the coffeehouse, began to teach me how to share the Gospel and to minister to people. It was through these years of discipleship that I became confident in sharing my faith and the Word. During the time I spent working with the coffeehouse (later renamed God's Army), I was equipped to share with people from all different kinds of religions, even cult members.

I was involved with this street ministry for five years. We were committed to sharing Christ. We would go out to minister during the week and on weekends—regardless of the weather. We witnessed on the streets, at big events in Casper, and at parades and county fairs in surrounding towns. We often wheeled a wooden cross up and down the main streets of Casper.

When I first gave my life to Christ, I was working at a grocery store. I wanted to be a witness for the Lord and prayed often that people would see Jesus in me. While I worked there, I would use my lunch and coffee breaks to share the Gospel with co-workers. I tried to share with as many people as I could about the wonderful things God was doing in my life. I wore a small pin on my apron that said, "Jesus Saves."

One day, after I had been wearing that pin for over a year, the store manager confronted me about it. He told me I had to take the pin off. I refused because several of the other workers wore t-shirts that had satanic messages on them. The store manager threatened to make me work the night shift if I didn't take it off. I still refused, and after several more threats, he backed down.

This was the first opposition I endured on my job for the cause of Christ, but it certainly would not be the last. God was using these early years in a small town in Wyoming to prepare me for a ministry to the nations of the world. Little did I know how soon this would all take place or the persecutions that would follow.

# Chapter 4

# DEATH TO ALL MISSIONARIES

"For if we live, we live for the Lord; or if we die, we die
for the Lord; therefore whether we live or die, we are
the Lord's" (Romans 14:8 NASB).

In 1983, three years after I was saved at the Don Francisco
concert, I began to sense God's call on my life to go to Israel
as a missionary. Growing up in Casper, a town of about 70,000
people, a weekend trip to Denver was a big thing for me.
So, God's call to leave my family and friends to go to Israel
indefinitely was a big step of faith. Since I was still young in

the faith, I needed many confirmations from the Lord to know that this was truly His will for me.

However, God is faithful, and somehow He orchestrated an opportunity for me to meet a lady in Casper named Babs. She had already been to Israel. She told me I should go live in Israel on a kibbutz, which is a communal-type farm. I asked the Lord to confirm whether it was His will for me to go to Israel: "If you really want me to go, please send someone today to tell me that I am supposed to go to Israel."

Later that day, a professor from the college I attended came through my check-out line at the grocery store and said, "I heard you are going to Israel."

"No, I'm not," I shot back.

"Yes, you are," he said.

"No, I'm not!"

To which he replied, "Yes, you are!" I questioned him as to how he knew this; he said a little bird had told him, then laughed, and walked away. I knew then that God really had orchestrated this whole situation and was directing my steps. So, I followed Bab's advice, made the arrangements, and set off for Israel.

Since it was my first trip overseas, there was a lot to do in preparation. I had to find a travel agent who could book a ticket with an open-ended return. Thankfully, the Lord led me to a sweet lady who had experience with travel to Israel. She helped direct me in preparing for the trip. Then I had to make a trip to Denver and meet with the Director of the organization that I would work under. Thankfully he gave me the green light to go, but told me that I was not allowed to share the Gospel with the Jewish people! I had planned to move to Israel indefinitely, so I had to pack all my things and store them.

While I was in Israel, I experienced some trying situations. However, the Lord used them to build my faith. They also gave me a heart to help the persecuted Church. I was the only Christian on a kibbutz of 700 people. For six weeks we had a few other Christians who came to live and work there, but otherwise I was alone in my faith.

My jobs at the kibbutz varied. I picked avocados and oranges for a few weeks. I also worked at a woodshop and in a shoe factory, but most of my time was spent in the kitchen preparing food and washing dishes.

I would often make weekend trips into Jerusalem where I would see signs on the telephone poles that read, "Death to all missionaries!" or, "All Christians are missionaries!"

At the age of 21, far away from my friends and family, I grew spiritually weary. But, I learned from my time in Israel that Jesus truly is my best friend and that He will never leave or forsake me. As a young Christian, I often prayed for faith for those in prison around the world. While praying for Christians in prison in Russia, the Lord showed me a picture of the Holy Spirit flooding the prison cell and the prisoners rejoicing before the Lord. I learned that the Holy Spirit is not bound by walls or prison bars.

While studying Hebrew on one kibbutz, I befriended a Jewish guy from New Jersey named Eddie. I shared the Gospel with him and I was able to pray with him for salvation. However, after I led him to Christ, I experienced a lot of opposition from the people on the kibbutz and also in Jerusalem at the Wailing Wall. Many people began to ignore me, while others openly mocked me. I ate many meals quietly by myself.

One day, while visiting Jerusalem, I was in the Upper Room. I met a man from Florida, who claimed to be a "Messianic believer." This is what they called Jewish followers of Jesus. While he and I talked, he convinced me to join a walking tour of the Jewish quarter of the old city. The man leading the tour was named Baruch; he was a radical Jew from New York City. I had met Baruch on a previous trip with Eddie. He had been very confrontational then.

I reluctantly joined the tour, and we went many miles into the Jewish quarter. We ended up in Baruch's apartment, which overlooked the Wailing Wall. Baruch sent around a clipboard to gather the names and addresses of the young Jewish people, intending to recruit them for conservative Jewish schools called yeshivas. The man who said he was a Jewish follower of Jesus got up and headed for the door. As he was leaving, he told Baruch that I was an evangelical missionary from the U.S. who came to convert Jews. I knew I was in trouble.

There I was, in a radical Jew's apartment in the Jewish quarter. I felt trapped and wondered if I would make it out alive. I prayed a desperate prayer, "Jesus, please help me!" The clipboard came to me and Baruch announced, "You don't need to fill that out." I said, "I think it's time for me to be going." I dismissed myself and prayed the whole way back to the Jaffa Gate.

During this time, I wondered if I would be thrown out of the country. For two weeks, I was in constant turmoil. Then a friend from back home sent me an encouraging letter. Once I read it, the Lord gave me the joy and strength to overcome my fears. I was able to press through and I no longer worried about what would happen. I finished out the semester and left the day after graduation to return to the United States.

Later, I found out that the man who presided over the school I attended died six weeks after graduation. This Jewish man had initially opposed me, thinking that my only reason for coming to Israel was to convert Jews to Christianity. But on the night of the graduation, my last night in Israel, he looked over at me and smiled. He knew I had been treated unjustly and that I was a good student; he respected my convictions. I felt like the Lord had used me to be a witness to this man, so he could see an example of biblical Christianity through my life.

Living in Israel was a defining experience for me and I knew when I came back to the U.S. that God had a plan for my life. Where it would take me, and how I would get there, would still be a mystery I'd have to discover.

# Chapter 5

# NO LONGER MY DESIRE—BUT GOD'S CALLING

"...you will be my witnesses in Jerusalem, and in all Judea and Samaria, and to the ends of the earth" (Acts 1:8b NIV).

After Israel, I returned to Casper and continued doing street ministry with God's Army. God continued to build my faith and develop in me the boldness to share my faith with anyone who crossed my path.

Then, in 1985, I tragically lost my best friend in a car

accident. At the time of his death, I had two options before me. I could either attend Kevin's funeral in Ohio or travel to a street ministries conference in Dallas, Texas. I was pretty shook up and felt it was not the time for me to go back for the funeral, so I decided to go to Dallas instead. It was a trip that would change the course of my life.

While I was at the conference, I met some students from Christ For The Nations Bible Institute (CFNI), an organization based there. Some of the students had recently been to Israel on a summer outreach from the school. As they shared about their experiences, I was very interested to find out more about CFNI. I enjoyed the praise and worship at the conference and the speakers truly lifted up the name of Jesus. My appetite was whet for Bible school.

After the conference, I returned to Wyoming and started to pray about attending CFNI. I was never one to want a lot of head knowledge or to attend seminary, but the Lord spoke to my heart that I would learn many practical lessons on how to apply the Word of God to my life if I went to school there. I sent in my application and six weeks later I received a call from the Dean of Men—I had been accepted. I promptly resigned my job and moved with some friends to Dallas, Texas.

God used the time at CFNI to give me a vision for the whole world. I fellowshipped, prayed, roomed and ate with students from all over the world. We also had national foreign workers and missionaries from different countries that came to speak and minister to us. All of them shared the needs on the mission field and requested that we pray about coming to help them one day. My heart was constantly being challenged to serve God in the foreign field.

This call to serve the Lord was very different from what I had heard back in Wyoming. There was no shortage of churches or need for more pastors back there. Here, the call was to go forth to the ripened fields of the world where the laborers were few. My heart was stirred as I heard about the incredible needs from all over the world. How could I stay at home, while so many were perishing around the world?

During my time at CFNI, my friends told me I was called to be a pastor. However, I found I had a passion for missions work and evangelism. So, even though I was studying to be a pastor, it was like trying to put a square peg in a round hole. After a lot of prayer, I visited the Academic Dean. I told him, "I would like to change my major from pastoral to missions." He said, "That's great! Where would you like to go as a missionary?"

At that time, I thought I would return to Israel after Bible College as a long-term missionary to the Jewish people. I told the Dean that I would like to go back to Israel and work there for the rest of my life. I did not know God had other plans for me. He said, "Okay, that's great, but you need to go to a third world country. You need to go to China."

I did not want to argue with him, but in the back of my mind I was thinking, *You don't understand ... I'm in Bible school. I'm struggling just to pay my school bill because my family doesn't financially support me. I have to completely trust God to provide for me. I'm working as hard as I can and it's all I can do to just pay my school bill, let alone find the money for a mission trip to China.* So, after talking to the Dean, I went to the Lord in prayer and asked, "Can I go to China?"

He said, "Pat, you see Me as you see your earthly father. You think that you have to work for everything that you get. Ask Me if you can go to China."

I said, "Lord, can I go to China?"

He replied, "Yes."

Then I thought, *Well, that was just too easy; that can't be God.*

I thought what I heard in prayer just couldn't be from God. So I said, "Lord, if this is really You, and You want me to go to China, please confirm it to me."

After praying, I went back to the men's dormitory and had lunch. When I checked my mailbox, there was a letter from the American Board of Missions to the Jews—a missions organization that reached out to the Jewish people. Imagine my shock at reading the front of the envelope: "First to the Jews, then to the Chinese." When I read this, I knew it was the confirmation from the Lord that I needed. Since I had already been to the Jews in Israel, I felt that God was saying that now was the time to go to the Chinese.

I asked the leader of the Asia outreach team how much

the trip would cost and she said $1,750.00. Even though it is not that much money today, it was a lot of money for me then. There were forty-three of us on the team who headed for China and Southeast Asia, and I was the only one who did not have the money.

At an outreach prayer meeting during lunchtime, my friend, Anna, said that the team should pray for my finances. Everyone prayed that God would provide for me to be a part of the outreach team. After praying, Anna said, "I feel like the Lord wants us to take up an offering to help Pat out." This was really humbling for me. These students, who were also going on the outreach, were now going to give money to me?

While preparing for the outreach, we had already seen incredible answers to our prayers. Some of the team members shared how their home churches were paying for half their trip, while others received calls from parents who were offering to pay their way. Meanwhile, I kept asking, "Have You forgotten me, Lord?" The 30 support letters I sent out had not generated much response.

The students took up an offering that day, which totaled about $118.00. I added that to my outreach bill. This was at 3:00 p.m. on Monday afternoon. I had until 4:00 p.m. to come up with enough money to buy my plane ticket. I was still short of the amount I needed by over $500.00. I had already missed two deadlines, and if I missed this one, I was off the team.

I went to my part-time job at the bank and battled with my thoughts. *Lord, did I really miss it? Did I presume that I should go to China?* My best friend was going to Amsterdam and they needed $536.00 for their down payment, the exact amount I had in my account. I thought that maybe I had missed the Lord. I wondered if I was supposed to go to Amsterdam. But as I prayed, I felt like I was still supposed to go to Southeast Asia.

The next morning, I got up early and went to seek the Lord in prayer. I spent time on my face … crying. Finally, I said, "Lord, I'm really sorry! I presumed rather than trusting You, and I am sorry. I thought You said I could go to China."

He said, "Pat, you asked if you could go to China. Now I'm asking you, will you go for Me?"

I knew then that God wanted to clarify something in my heart. Before, it was a desire of mine to go to China. That desire had to die that morning, so that God could resurrect my calling to China as His ambassador. No longer was it my desire, but rather God's calling. In prayer, I said, "Yes, Lord, I'll go for You!"

After spending an hour with the Lord, I went to the early Tuesday morning prayer meeting at 7:00. Unfortunately, the enemy began to play tricks with my mind. He kept telling me, "Pat, you're really stupid. Everybody knows you don't have the money. They are laughing at you. Why don't you quit? Why don't you just give up, quit, and forget about the trip?"

In my mind I said, "Satan, I am going to keep pressing on." Three times I almost left the prayer meeting, but each time I decided to stay and trust the Lord to work out my financial situation.

At 9:30 that morning, I went to the Finance Office with two good friends to see what was going on with my account. When we got there, I told the secretary my name and that I wanted to check to see how much was on my account. She looked up the file and said, "It's paid—you're going!" I shouted, "What?!"

She just smiled and said, "Yes, you had $700.00 come in yesterday." This meant that I had $1,236.00, which was more than enough to pay for the airplane ticket. I jumped, screamed, and yelled from one building to the other—I couldn't believe it! Like manna from Heaven, the Lord really came through for me with just what I needed at exactly the right time.

My faith grew that day as I began to learn how to trust the Lord like never before. I found out later that the leader of the outreach had sensed the Lord prompting her to put some money into my account because one day I would end up working as a long-term missionary in Southeast Asia.

After that, the Lord began to provide in a lot of interesting ways. At the bank, I was working as a teller at the drive-through window. I had several Christians come to my window and tell me the Lord told them to give me money. The bank's Southern Baptist vice-president donated $100.00 for me to go preach the Gospel. My home church in Casper sent $600.00 the day before I left. God poured out His blessings on me—I had more than enough money to go.

God also provided for my other needs along the way.

Someone had given me three suits. A few weeks before the summer break, a friend of mine said he would not be going to the graduation banquet because he did not have a suit to wear. I had him try on one of the suits I had been given; it fit him great, so I gave it to him.

A couple of weeks later, when I was getting ready to go on the trip, I had been praying for some shorts and t-shirts. A friend of a friend of mine called and said he had a bunch of clothes I might like. When I drove over to his house to pick up the clothes, they filled the whole front of my pickup. There were four or five pairs of shorts, about a dozen shirts, a couple of suits, and a dozen pairs of pants—it was incredible!

I believe that because I was obedient to give a suit away to my friend who was in need, God in turn blessed me. Another need I had was for a camera. One day, out of the blue, somebody who did not know that I needed a camera gave me one.

The day came to leave Dallas for the outreach. We went to South Korea first, and I found it overwhelming to be surrounded by a sea of Asian faces. For the first time in my life, I was a minority. But God's compassion for the people of Asia began to rise up in my heart. After visiting Dr. Yonggi Cho's church and Prayer Mountain in Seoul, we traveled on to Hong Kong. From there, we crossed the border into China to take in the Bibles we had brought with us. It happened to be my birthday and I was excited.

For the border crossing, I was teamed up with two friends,

a guy and a girl. When we arrived at the border, the girl just ignored the Customs agent and walked right through the checkpoint. My other friend got stopped, and then they called me over and asked if I had Bibles. I denied that I did—I lied.

The Customs agent said, "Open your bag." He opened my bag and immediately saw the Bibles, which he confiscated. I felt pretty low because I had lied, and it was on my birthday, and on my first trip to take Bibles into a "closed" country. I asked the Lord to forgive me for lying. Finally, the agents let us go and we joined the rest of the team.

My responsibility now was to go into the bathroom and switch the Bibles that had made it through into different bags for storage. The girl on my team had made it through with quite a few Bibles, and my other friend and I were wearing Bibles on our bodies that they had missed.

The bathroom I was using for the bag switch had "squatty potties," which are basically a hole in the floor. As you can imagine, the floors were covered with urine and the smell on that hot summer day was enough to make me want to throw up. In the humidity, my clothes stuck to me and I could feel myself sweating on the Bibles underneath my clothes.

I squeezed into a stall and balanced the bags on my shoes to keep them off the floor. Holding my breath as much as possible, I managed to repack the Bibles with clothes all around them. My heart was pounding so hard, I was sure the others could hear it. Finally, I got all the Bibles packed up and we stored them for our contacts to pick up later. Having accomplished what we came for, we returned to Hong Kong.

The next day, I made another border crossing and this time I got through with no problems. It was a thrill to simply walk through Customs, and I suddenly knew this was what I was created to do. I love delivering Bibles to people! It has been a tremendous joy for me, from that day until now. I truly believe that giving people the Bible is the best thing I can do.

So the mission trip was a huge success, not only for the missions we wanted to accomplish, but for the peace it brought me in knowing what I wanted to do for the Lord with my life. We returned to Dallas, grateful for all we had seen the Lord do through us for His people in China.

Now, school was about to end. As I prepared to graduate, I sensed the call of God on my life to be a full-time missionary, but I was concerned about where I was to go. I prayed for direction, but it seemed God was silent. So I kept praying, asking God for clear direction as to where I was to serve and what He would have me do there.

One night, I was visiting my best friend who oversaw the men's dormitory. A man came to the room complaining of chest pains. He thought it might be a heart attack, so we took him to the emergency room at a local hospital. Happily, everything checked out fine.

But as we were leaving, I saw an older lady in a wheelchair. I felt the Lord's prompting to go over and pray for her. I approached her and asked if I could pray for her. She was elated, so we laid our hands on her shoulders and began to pray. Afterwards, she pointed at me and said, "Young man, God is getting ready to take you to many places and very soon." God used this precious saint to encourage me when I least expected it—at 2:30 in the morning in the emergency room.

The next week I went to visit the children's pastor at the church I attended in Dallas. While I worked with the children's ministry, I had become friends with this pastor, so I asked him to pray for me to receive direction in what I should do after I graduated. While we prayed together, he said the Lord gave him a vision. In the vision he saw me going from country to country. He told me that he had never seen pictures before as he prayed, so I knew the Lord was confirming what He had already put in my heart to do.

Amazingly, as God has unfolded His plan for my life, I have seen this vision coming to pass. I have been able to see teams go all over the world, bringing God's precious Word to hungry people and to those who are persecuted for their faith. My first journeys, into Israel and China, stirred up my passion for the lost nations. During the next few years, I began to see God unfold his plan for my life, one small step at a time. But first, there was still more schooling I had to complete.

# Chapter 6

# TRAVELING TO NORTHWEST CHINA

"The wicked man flees though no one pursues, but the righteous are as bold as a lion" (Proverbs 28:1 NIV).

After graduating from Christ For The Nations, I did some traveling, but soon realized I needed to finish my bachelor's degree. At that time, CFNI could only provide a certificate and I felt that God wanted me to have more education before going into full-time missions work.

So I moved to Southern California to attend Vanguard University, which was called Southern California College at the time. It was a Christian school and I was able to continue growing in my faith with other believers while I finished my studies. Finally, in 1990, I graduated.

After praying, I felt the Lord was leading me back to China to minister to unreached people. I would need to work as an English teacher in order to get a visa to live inside the country. I returned first to Hong Kong since I had been there previously with CFNI, and felt led to contact a missions organization that placed missionaries inside China. They asked me where in China I was hoping to go. I told them I wanted to go to Beijing so I could study Mandarin for two years. After that, I wanted to go to Northwest China.

A few years earlier, I had heard about a minority people group there known as the Uyghurs. There were just five missionaries working among five million people. I was really burdened for them, and I had a strong desire now to go to Northwest China to work with them in any way that I could.

To my surprise, the missions agency had an opening in Northwest China. I could immediately go there, study the Mandarin language, teach English, and work with the Uyghur people. I thought it was an answer to prayer and became excited.

A few days later, I took the train and headed into northern China. I rode the train for nearly five days before I could stop to rest and visit an old friend. I spent two days in Xian and it was a much needed break in the journey.

When I finally arrived in Northwest China, I learned that there were now fifty missionaries working in the area. I was warned by some of them right from the start that I needed to be very careful and not share the Gospel. Apparently, the last missionary, a lady who had been at the school where I would be teaching, was almost kicked out because she was sharing the Gospel.

I love to share the Gospel—it is one of my favorite things to do. God has blessed and anointed me to share His message of salvation. But right from the beginning when I started working with these people, I felt a spirit of fear come over me. This fear gripped me for three weeks. During that time, I did not share the Gospel at all. I knew this was not God's will, for the spirit of fear was sent from the enemy to paralyze me, but I could not seem to shake the dread that continued to hang over me.

Finally, I decided I'd had enough. I told the Lord that I was going to pass out one booklet, the Gospel of Mark in the Uyghur dialect, and the consequences were up to Him. I was very excited to go out—nervous—but excited! As I walked around the city, I kept praying and praying. I knew I had to pass out that one booklet if I was ever going to get victory over the fear.

After several hours, I went into a shopping center we called the "Pink Mall." As I walked around, I saw a young Uyghur lady, obviously from a Muslim background judging from her dress, and I thought to myself, *I need to give her the Gospel of Mark.* I bought something from the stand where she was working and I gave her the Gospel booklet. She seemed genuinely excited to receive it and I was so thankful for a victory over my fear.

The next day, I prayed again and thought I would give away two booklets this time. Again I headed out, walked around the city, and prayed for the Lord's guidance. I had to ride a bus to get where I wanted to go.

When I got off the bus, right away I saw a lady and her son, who were also Muslims. I approached them, but even before I could offer her the booklet, the lady cried out, "Isa,

Isa." This is how they say "Jesus" among the Uyghurs. She knew what this booklet was, even before I gave it to her, and was thrilled to get it. Later, I gave the second book out to a Muslim man. Again, I was so excited to have victory over the fear.

On the third day, I decided to go back out again and this time I would give away three booklets. As I did this, I found that I was met with such a warm reception to the Gospel. People were very eager to receive this booklet and to hear the truth of Jesus Christ. I kept doing this. On the fifth day, I finally felt the oppression break off of me. I was then free to share the Gospel and to minister to my students.

I had a Chinese teacher named Ma Jun, who was an amiable man. He was not only my teacher, but also a good friend. The government decided to sponsor a trip around the province for foreign teachers—as a kind of propaganda—and Ma Jun went as a guide. My friend, Tom, and I were able to share the Gospel with him during the trip and he was very receptive.

When we returned to the city, I sensed the Lord saying this was the day of Ma Jun's salvation. I told God, "Okay, Lord, I'm here. If you want me to pray with him, I will be more than glad to do that. But please have him come to talk to me."

At about eight o'clock that evening, there was a knock on my apartment door. I knew before I even opened the door who would be standing there; sure enough, it was Ma Jun. I welcomed him in and we chatted for a bit. I finally decided to wade into more spiritual waters with our conversation.

I had been praying at that time about a lady back in the United States that I was interested in. I told him, "Ma Jun, I am going to pray about this girl and ask the Lord about this relationship, to see if it is God's will or not. Would you pray in agreement with me?"

He said, "Yes, but I do not know how to pray."

"Well, I'll pray and you just agree with me," I said.

He said, "Okay."

I prayed and told him to say "Amen," which he did. Then I said, "Ma Jun, I believe the Lord has told me that today is your day; you are ready to receive the Gospel, to accept Jesus Christ as your Lord and Savior, and to repent of your sins."

He said, "Yes, I am."

That night I was able to pray with him to receive Jesus as his Lord and Savior. About a month later, his wife also became a Christian. She had witnessed the change in her husband. It was a joy for me to see them both come to know Christ!

A missionary friend of mine, also working in China, taught me how to use parables in my English classes to convey the truths of the Bible, so I often used parables to spark curiosity. Several times after class, my students would ask me about the true meaning of those stories. Then, when they would come for talks in my private residence, I would share the Gospel freely.

Two of my Chinese students came to my apartment for

one of my talks. I thought, *You're on my turf now, and I can openly share the Gospel*. Both of these young men gave their hearts to the Lord and I spent a couple of months discipling them. They were so excited to know about Jesus that they brought two more of their friends. Eventually, their friends also became Christians. The four of these young men were very humble and teachable. It was both a privilege and a joy to baptize them, which we did in the bathtub! Then, I continued discipling them in their faith.

I also had the privilege of sharing the Gospel with three young Muslim men and they became Christians, too. I worked with these young Uyghurs and tried to disciple them. I have since heard that one of them has become a pastor in Northwest China. Another one has worked on the Uyghur translation of the Bible. What an encouragement to see fruit like this!

When I moved to Northwest China, I would often go for walks in the city. I would pass a mosque, which stirred my heart with prayers for the Gospel to go forth. I would pray, "Lord, You know that some people in America want a Mercedes-Benz and other people want diamond rings, but Lord, I don't want those things. What I would like to see is that all the people of this mosque come to know You as their Lord and Savior." That was my prayer.

I asked, and kept asking, "Lord, please grant this desire of my heart." I would walk around the mosque, praying for the people inside to come to know Jesus—for the truth of the Word and Who He was to penetrate their hearts.

I learned that about fifty years before, this particular city had been badly flooded. People flocked to the spiritual diviners to find out how to prevent another catastrophe like this. The chief diviner told them that the two hills outside of the city were the back of a dragon, which guarded the city. His back was broken, so the people should build a pagoda on each hill and dedicate the city to the dragon. Naturally, they followed these instructions and when I arrived, there were two stately pagodas that presided over the city from those hilltops.

One day, I decided to go up to these high places with a couple of like-minded friends to pray for the city. We said, "Lord, this city belongs to You. It does not belong to the dragon." We saw the dragon as a symbol of Satan, so we told God that the city did not belong to the dragon; it belonged to Him and all the people in it. We climbed to the top of one of the hills and worshipped the Lord—singing, praying, and reading Scriptures together. At other times, I would go to the other hill by myself and pray that the Lord would bring down the strongholds in that city.

Then, one time, I said, "Lord, it's not enough that I just pray. I want to do something to help bring down the stronghold." So I decided that every time I went up there, I would pull a few rocks out from underneath the pagoda. My hope was that one day the pagoda would become unstable and just tumble down the side of the hill. I was praying and reading Scripture aloud with my Bible open.

After about an hour, several Chinese soldiers came

walking up the hill. I was just sitting there reading the Word of God, but I could sense there was a clash in the Spirit with one of these soldiers. He must have known I was a Christian because of my Bible. Two of the soldiers were curious and asked me what the book was. I told them it was a Bible and that I was a Christian. I started sharing the Gospel with them, and the other soldier became visibly upset. I could tell he did not like it, but I continued because the others were interested.

After a little while, they asked me if I would take some pictures of them. Then, while I was taking their pictures in different poses, they asked me to be in a picture with them. I agreed, and while my arms were around their shoulders, I prayed for their salvation. Posing with them would turn out to be a mistake, though.

I descended the hill about 10 minutes later, but continued to sense the one soldier was irate because the other two had been receptive to Christ. However, I returned to my apartment on the college campus.

My friend, Marilyn, and I went out for dinner shortly after this. We walked down the back hallways and exited through the front door. As we left the building, we saw two men standing there, talking by the bushes outside of one of the windows. It was rather strange. I called Marilyn's attention to it and we both started to quietly pray.

One of the men ran out from the bushes and stopped about fifteen feet in front of us. He stood there staring at us for a moment, and then suddenly dashed back into the bushes. His partner ran out, stopped about ten feet in front of us—then did the same thing and returned to the bush. Now, we were really praying! Since they were not stopping us, we kept walking and continued on to dinner.

The next day I saw Marilyn and we prayed together again. She said, "What do you think about those men we saw in the bushes last night?"

I said, "I don't know."

She said, "The Scripture says that the righteous are as bold as a lion, but the wicked flee when no one is pursuing them. Pat, you are being followed by the secret police, but you don't need to be afraid because God is with you."

Two weeks after meeting those soldiers, I was called into the vice president's office at the school. Unlike the president of the college, who appeared to favor me, I knew the vice-president was less fond of me. He seemed suspicious of foreigners in general, but there had also always seemed to be a clash between us. I knew it was because he was opposed to the Gospel.

At the meeting, he said, "The reason for our meeting today is because I have heard you've been preaching the Gospel." Then he asked me, "Patrick, are you preaching the Gospel in your classes?"

I said, "No, I am not preaching the Gospel in my classes."

He said, "This is China. You cannot preach religion here. It is against the law."

"I am a Christian and I am not ashamed to tell people that.

You hired me to teach English and American culture, and that is what I teach my students. In my free time, yes, I do share about Jesus."

He said, "If you want to stay here, you cannot preach about Jesus any more. If you will give me your word that you will not talk about Jesus any more, we will let you stay."

"Sir," I said, "I am not going to lie to you. I have to tell people about Jesus. He has forgiven my sins. He has given me a new life. I have to tell people about Him! It would be wrong if I didn't tell them."

He said, "If you'll just promise not to talk about Jesus any more, we will let you stay."

"No," I said, "I can't make that promise. I have to obey the Lord Jesus. The Bible says, 'Go into all the world and preach the Gospel,' so that's what I'm doing."

"But you can't keep preaching the Gospel and stay here," he said.

"Well, then, I'll leave."

He said, "No, no; you don't have to leave. We don't want you to go. We just want you to not talk about Jesus."

I said, "I just can't do that. I have to talk to people about Jesus."

He realized that I would not compromise, so he said, "Okay. When are you leaving?"

I said, "I'm leaving Sunday afternoon at four o'clock."

He said, "How are you leaving?"

I said, "I am going by train."

He said, "Okay. Now I need you to write out a confession of your crime."

I began by writing that when I was a child, my father taught me that I was always to tell the truth. My heavenly Father also says I am to tell the truth, so I was telling people the truth, which is that God loves them and Satan hates them. Satan wants to take people to hell, but God wants to take them to Heaven, if they repent of their sins and trust Jesus as their Lord and Savior. Instead of confessing my crime, I shared the Gospel again.

For some reason, the vice president accepted the paper I wrote. Now that I was leaving, I needed to say goodbye to my new brothers in Christ. During that last week, the secret police followed me everywhere. I quickly learned how to outsmart them by walking fast down side streets and ducking down alleyways. I found I could always lose them. In this way, I could meet with the new Christians I was discipling to tell them that I was leaving China, but I would pray for them. Although it was difficult to say goodbye to those I ministered to, I felt it was best to go. I certainly did not want to endanger their lives or their relationship with Jesus.

On Sunday morning, I was all packed up and ready to go back to Hong Kong. During prayer that morning, the Holy Spirit impressed on me that I was supposed to leave early. The word came: "Go Early." I walked down to the school where Marilyn was because I knew the police were following me. I could not go to the railway station to get a new ticket without being tailed, so I asked Marilyn to go for me. The new ticket she bought was for an 11:00 a.m. departure.

At 10:00 a.m., I headed out for the railway station. For some reason, the police were not waiting for me. I guess they planned to get me Sunday afternoon at 4:00 p.m. I boarded the train on time and left with no problems. Later, Marilyn told me the police were at the station at 4:00 p.m. to arrest me. I thank God that I was on the train before they knew it and was safely on my way to Hong Kong.

Since that time, I have been back to that university city about five times. Each time, I carried literature with me to help strengthen our brothers and sisters in the Lord and to reach out to the lost. God has begun a good work and He will carry it on to completion.

My heart is still burdened for the Uyghur people, so it was with great joy that I could lead a team back there in 1994. There were 17 of us on that team. We flew from Singapore to Pakistan, and from there we traveled by road from Islamabad up to Skardu. Then we crossed over the Khakoram Pass with about 10,000 copies of the Gospel of Mark in the Uyghur dialect. We also had about 4,000 Uyghur tracts called, "The Righteous Road," which have been particularly effective in reaching Muslims with the Gospel.

During this trip, most of our team had made it through Customs, but the last two people were stopped. When the Gospel literature was discovered, the agents hauled all of us back in. Over the next few hours, they confiscated all the books and asked lots of questions.

A taxi driver who was waiting at the station asked me, "What did you do?"

I said, "We brought in books."

"What kind of books?"

"Parts of the Bible," I said.

"You can't bring Bibles in here," he said, "We're Muslims."

I said, "Well, we brought Bibles in here."

He acted like he was upset with us, but asked, "Could I have one, please?" We gave one to him.

The head Customs agent who was questioning us asked the team leader, "Why do you bring in all these books?"

He said, "Because we're Christians and we love the Muslim people. We've been praying for the Muslim people and came to bring the Good News to them. We heard that in your culture it is good to bring a gift, so we brought lots of gifts for lots of people."

They asked, "Who are you going to give these to?"

"Well," he replied, "just to people in general. We are traveling through Northwest China and we'd like to distribute these."

The agent in charge said, "I can't believe you would spend all this money to have all this literature printed—and then bring a group this far, halfway around the world, to bring this to us." Our team leader said, "We do it because Jesus loves you."

This man was dumbfounded that we would do such a thing. It was a great opportunity to minister the Gospel to the man who was the head of Customs. They did confiscate the literature, which we later heard was sold on the black market; the government distributed it for us. We praised the Lord for that work. In the Book of Philippians, Paul writes: "The important thing is that in every way, whether from false motives or true, Christ is preached. In this I rejoice" (Philippians 1:18). That is how we felt about getting the Gospel out to the people.

Back in the same city where I had taught before, I decided to take the team up to one of those high places. Unfortunately, despite my rock-robbing efforts, the pagoda still stood there. About nine of us went down to pray at "my" mosque, but it was closed when we arrived. I told the team to just walk in front of it and pray. While we were walking and praying, somebody came to the gate. They asked if we would like to come in and see the mosque.

I said, "You bet we would." They opened the gate and invited us inside. We took off our shoes as a sign of respect, which is required in mosques. Inside, we walked around and prayed that God would reveal Himself to the Muslim people when they came to worship. Then we were invited into a separate room for tea and watermelon.

We said, "Can we sing a song for you?" They agreed. We sang several songs and then we sang a song called, "No Other Name, but the Name of Jesus." We had our hands raised worshipping the Lord. One of the Muslim men had tears in his eyes. He could sense the Presence of God in that room.

After the head of the mosque (the Imam) joined us, we sat and talked with him for a while. Marilyn started to share with him about their practice of sacrificing a lamb. She talked about Jesus, the Lamb of God, who died on the cross for our sins. She asked this man, "Have you ever read the Uyghur New Testament?"

He said, "No, it's not in our language." He did not know that it was being translated right then, but there were portions of it that had been finished. He said, "If it were translated, I would really like to read it."

These men let us pray for them. We made a circle around them, laid our hands on them, and prayed aloud. We prayed that the Truth would be revealed to them and that God would bless them. As we were leaving, Marilyn slipped the Imam a copy of the Gospel of Mark in the Uyghur dialect. He was very grateful for it.

I believe that in Heaven, I am going to see a lot of people from that city—converted Muslims and converted Muslim leaders, who have been reached by black market Gospel tracts. I know our prayers at the pagoda have not gone unanswered!

# Chapter 7

# ONE CLOSED DOOR LEADS
# TO MANY OPEN ONES

"He who is faithful in what is least is faithful also
in much ..." (Luke 16:10a NKJV).

All of this really started for me after I graduated from
college. By 1991, I was teaching English in northern China
and sharing my faith whenever the opportunity arose. When
the school asked me to stop sharing my faith, even on my own
time, I knew I couldn't agree to this and made the decision to
leave.

I felt as though I had totally failed God. When I was a
young Christian, I had read many books about missionaries

who had given their all. They left their home countries and settled in foreign lands for the rest of their lives. This is what I had planned for my life—to give my all for China. Like the missionaries of old who packed their belongings in coffins when they sailed overseas, I thought this was the way to do it. However, God's plans are not always our plans … and today, I'm so glad they aren't!

After I left China, I returned to Hong Kong. I started leading teams into China on a daily basis, carrying much needed Bibles to the growing church. It was experiencing tremendous growth at that time, too, and there was a great need for God's Word.

After several months of leading teams with heavy loads of Bibles, some friends asked me to go to Vietnam, Laos, and Cambodia with them. Carrying thousands of pieces of Gospel literature into Vietnam in 1991 was quite an experience. We also distributed literature throughout Cambodia and carried our first load of Lao New Testaments into the poor country of Laos.

I remember boarding a small boat which carried us across the Mekong River—once again unsure of what lay ahead, but knowing we were in God's hands. The Customs formality was very easy and we sailed through unscathed. Truly our prayers had been answered!

The hunger for God's Word in these countries was immense. Bringing in a small load of precious books to spiritually feed them was rewarding, but also challenging. A one-time delivery would simply not meet the need. It became clear to me that this was an ongoing need and delivering Bibles to closed countries was something God was calling me to do—in fact, something that He was asking me to dedicate my life to! It was confirmation of what I had felt on my first trip to China.

One day, while living in Hong Kong, I felt impressed by the Lord to minister to some Nepalese Gurkha soldiers. I found out they already had a Bible study going, so I joined them. We instantly became friends and one of them invited me to Nepal. I prayed about it for a year and a half. Then, in 1993, I sensed it was the Lord's timing for me to go. I asked the Lord to provide a contact to work with once I arrived. On the flight over, I sensed the Lord was saying that I was to reach out to the Sherpas.

The day that I arrived in Kathmandu, I was blessed to see the Himalayas. The country truly is beautiful. However, the trip from the airport to the tourist area can create sensory overload: gurus wearing just loincloths, cows with "attitudes" walking down the middle of streets, constant honking (a traffic courtesy in Nepal), and the clutter of motorbikes, cycles, double-decker buses, and pedestrians all vying for space.

That night I was invited to dinner at the home of a man who is reaching the Himalayan region with the Gospel. We quickly became friends and I sensed God's providence in this meeting. Then he began to share about the work he was doing in the northern part of Nepal among the Sherpas.

When he said "Sherpa," my ears perked up. I shared with him what God had spoken to me on the airplane about helping the Sherpas. He then invited me to go with him for several days to minister to these people. I could clearly see the hand of God in this "chance" meeting.

We made the 75 mile, 10-hour bus ride up to the village. The buses in Nepal are unlike our luxury coaches in America. People bring their chickens, goats, ducks and sheep on the bus. The first class seats are in the bus, while the second class seats are on top of the bus—with air-conditioning and a 360 degree view, as our contact would say!

Since people are not supposed to ride on the top of buses in Nepal, the driver stops 50 feet before the police check point. The people climb down and the bus drives through the checkpoint. Afterwards, they climb back on top of the bus again. In this way, the police can say the bus didn't come through with people on top of it.

The mountains in Nepal are spectacular, and seeing the villages gives one a true perspective of life in Nepal that you don't get in Kathmandu. In the villages, life is much simpler. The people are also friendlier and more hospitable.

We got off the bus and made the four hour trek to our destination. Towering mountain peaks over 22,000 feet high overshadowed this beautiful Sherpa village. The border with Tibet was "only a three day walk" for a local, while for me it would take about five days.

The mountain village was breathtaking—a community of

400 people scattered across the ridge of the mountain, not far from Langtang Mountain that looms over 23,000 feet high. The Lord granted me favor with the Sherpa people and I was able to minister to the leader of the congregation. It is beautiful to hear the Sherpa people sing praises to Jesus in their native language. They sing in rounds, and it echoes through the mountains, lifting praises to our God and King.

Today, some 20 years later, through our relationship with this Nepalese family, Vision Beyond Borders has been able to serve the poor, care for orphans, minister to victims of human trafficking, and share the Gospel with those who are unreached. Tens of thousands of pounds of clothes, medical supplies, medicines, vitamins, and vegetable seeds have been brought in to help the poor.

God has blessed the ministry to support multiple Christian children's homes and to build two new ones. There are currently over 100 children whose physical, spiritual, and educational needs are being met through sponsorship. We're constructing several Christian schools and have funded two water projects to bring water to over 200 families.

Work is also being done to rescue and rehabilitate women and girls from sex trafficking. We support a beauty salon outreach in the red-light district that's dedicated to ministering to these precious women and rescuing those ready to escape. We just opened an additional safe house to care for trafficked victims and provide vocational training so they can learn skills to effectively support themselves and their families.

We also work with indigenous missionaries and children's workers in the homes. One of the homes we support was started by a pastor. He travels to Tibet to share the Gospel in remote villages and often encounters orphaned children. He started bringing them back and opened a Children's Home to care for them. These children love to sing and worship Jesus in their native Tibetan tongue. They have also been active in reaching out to the local Tibetan community.

One time, as this pastor was traveling to rescue children and share the Gospel in Tibet, the word spread about what he was doing. A Sherpa man from a strong Buddhist village tried to kill him in a drunken rage. The pastor ducked when this man tried to stab him and the knife hit a monk instead, cutting his hand badly. The pastor asked for forgiveness from the monk, who was moved by the gesture and came to Christ.

Thirteen families in the village have now come to know Jesus as their Savior. All of this happened as the result of an unfortunate incident! The pastor is now hoping to build a church in this Tibetan village.

It is incredible to witness the devotion of such faithful servants of Christ, like this pastor. They willingly give of themselves and lay their lives down to ensure others have an opportunity to hear the Truth of the Gospel. Despite persecution, oppression, and the hardships they face—they are undeterred in bringing the Gospel to their people. It is an honor and privilege to come alongside them, encourage them, and to help supply some of their needs!

Years ago, we asked our contact's ministry staff how we could help them. They requested hand wind tape players so they could reach people in the villages in their own dialects. They had 155 villages that were waiting for these players. Nepal has over 150 languages and dialects. A friend and I took the first load in, which consisted of 44 players. Although we were stopped at Customs, they only looked at the players and then let us go with all of our supplies.

The next team carried in 100 players. The staff was so encouraged that one of them began to jump for joy! In Nepal, many of the people in the villages are illiterate. There's no electricity and batteries are often hard to find or expensive. As a result, the hand wind tape players have been a very effective tool to use in reaching people with the Gospel.

In one village, a young Hindu man heard the Gospel for the first time. He was convicted by the Holy Spirit, repented of his sins, and put his faith and trust in Jesus Christ. His family kicked him out of the house for becoming a Christian, but he took the player and has played the Gospel cassette for over 1,000 people. We have heard reports of whole villages coming to faith in Christ as a result of the hand wind tape players.

To date, our teams have been blessed to deliver over 10,000 players to this ministry in Nepal. We are now bringing in hand wind CD players, in order to reach even more people with the Gospel. God is using these players all over the Himalayan region to further His Kingdom and to break the strongholds of

Hinduism and Buddhism. The staff has reported that through the large numbers of players being delivered to their country, their ministry has really grown!

When we bring teams to Nepal, we always visit the Hindu and Buddhist Temples, and if possible, bring them to the local church services. It's easy to see the hope, joy and truth of Christianity as it stands in stark contrast to the darkness, despair, futility, and hopelessness of these false religions.

It is heart-breaking to witness loved ones bringing their family members to the Hindu Temple as they are dying. They place the dying person's feet in the filthy Ganges River. This provides a false hope that if they die with their feet in the water, it will wash away their sins and give them a better reincarnation. Family members often scoop up the stinky water and pour it into their loved ones mouths, even as they are dying.

As we watch, we sense the oppression and hopelessness. These people seem to understand that they are not ready to face a Holy God. They seem to sense that they are unclean and need to be cleansed. However, they do not know that this filthy water is not what can cleanse them; it is only Jesus, who died and paid the penalty for their sins! They do not know that He is their only hope and through His blood they can be white as snow!

The Buddhist Temples have big gongs that people hit as they arrive. This is done to try and get their gods to notice them. They spin prayer wheels as they pray, hoping their prayers will reach their gods. It is as if they sense their prayers are hindered, but they do not know why. They do not understand that it's through Jesus we can approach the throne of God with freedom and confidence.

As we visit these temples, I am reminded of the incredible truth of Christ—and the futility and hopelessness of approaching God in any way *other* than through the atoning blood of Jesus Christ. They need to know the true God who can hear their prayers if they sincerely cry out for His mercy, and we must understand the urgency that exists to share that truth with those who are perishing outside of Him.

We are committed to getting God's Word to people and showing them the message of the true, living God—to offer them hope by preaching good news, binding up the broken-hearted, proclaiming freedom for the captives, and releasing prisoners from the darkness of false religion! It is our desire to see them with a garment of praise instead of a spirit of despair!

One young girl that was rescued from a very difficult situation is Maggie. She was from far west Nepal. Her mom is a deaf-mute and believed to be mentally handicapped. Maggie's beginning was tragic. She was born out of wedlock, the product of rape. When our contact met her in a village, she was sitting on a box with flies all over her face. She could not walk or talk at 6 years old.

Her mother was an outcast, from the lowest caste, and she had the job of cleaning out cow sheds with her bare hands.

Even though she washed her hands, she still had manure on them when she fed bread to her daughter. They were so poor they couldn't even afford a cup; they drank tea off a plate. Maggie crawled on all fours into the cow shed, where they lived with the animals.

Our contact asked her mother if he could take her to Kathmandu to get her an education and a better life; the mother agreed. It cost $200.00 to hire a man to make the eight hour hike up the mountain and carry her the eight hours back down the mountain—on his back. He then took her 26 hours by bus to Kathmandu, where she lived with the contact's family for a couple of weeks. She ate continuously because she was so malnourished. Within two weeks, she was saying "mama" and "daddy" after being around his kids. She was then moved to a children's home where she learned how to walk and talk. Now she's a normal little girl who has excelled in school and loves Jesus.

Another child was found in a garbage can when he was only three weeks old—he was blue. The mother had just thrown him away. The doctor said he would either die or have severe brain damage from oxygen deprivation, but the house parents said, "We're going to pray for him." They did pray for him and God healed him. As a little boy, he would hang on the director's leg and was the apple of his eye! Now he's grown up, attends high school, and loves sports.

Kevin was also abandoned when he was little. He lost his father at a very young age. When he was five years old, his mother took him to a restaurant and left him there to work. She never returned. He was made to wash the dishes, and after some time, the owners made him hand wash their clothes as well. Then they stopped feeding him, so he ran away. He lived on the streets until a policeman found him and brought him to the Children's Home. He was only six years old at the time. He is now a handsome eleven-year-old young man. He loves Jesus and likes to play soccer. He wants to be a policeman when he grows up, so he can bring other homeless kids to live in the Children's Home.

Each of the kids has their own unique story. It's encouraging to spend time with them and let them know how much they matter. We visit that particular home every time we go to Nepal. When they wanted a bat and balls, we brought it to them and played baseball in the field next door. We play soccer, volleyball, and other games together. It's been a joy to my heart to see the kids grow up, and I'm Uncle Pat to them. God has blessed me and I'm thankful to be able to do what I can to help kids around the world.

Once, I was with my friend Gary from the 700 Club. We were walking in the tourist area, along with a team. We were on our way to dinner when we saw some street kids—we both looked at the kids and then at each other. We decided we would stop to minister to them after dinner. Street children are usually treated like trash by the locals because they beg from the tourists. They often sniff glue that has been squeezed into bags to try to escape their bleak reality and suffering. It truly saddens me to see their lack of hope and vision.

After dinner, we stopped at a store and bought them some sandwiches. They wanted ketchup and mustard on them, which I thought was really cute! So we went back into the store to put ketchup and mustard on them. Normally, the local people don't like the street kids coming into their store, but we brought them in with us. The kids were dirty, and they had probably been sniffing glue, but Jesus would have befriended them if He were walking the Earth today.

We wanted to know their stories. The boys were Raju and Sankar, and there was a young girl as well. They spoke English because they were around tourists. Raju's dad had died and his mom couldn't afford to support him. Sankar's dad was an alcoholic who beat him, so he ran away from home. They thought they would go to Kathmandu to make money. Life on the streets is not easy and there are many temptations with drugs, alcohol, and now, even tourists who are using the kids for sex.

We had a good time sharing with them about Jesus. We prayed for them before we left, and afterwards, we both had a burden to continue praying for them. While visiting one of the children's homes a few months later, we saw them at the home. They stayed for two weeks and then decided life on the streets was better with more freedom, no schooling, and no structure. They could make money on the streets, smoke, and do whatever they wanted. So, they went back to the streets.

It is difficult for us to imagine that anyone who was given

a choice would choose this kind of lifestyle, but there's a lot of spiritual warfare involved in rescuing children who have been discarded, who have suffered such extreme abuse, and have been left to survive on their own. There are deep root issues of not feeling lovable, or even deserving of love, so they struggle with the boundaries of real love. They have believed these lies and are in great need of their eyes to be opened to the Truth. They need a revelation of God's love for them.

One day, I was downtown with a team and saw Raju and Sankar. I told them, "Go back to the Children's Home." That same day, Sankar decided he didn't want to live on the streets anymore; he didn't want that lifestyle. He decided he would rather be in the Christian home and that he wanted to get an education so he could have a chance in life.

When we went back to the Children's Home that night, Sankar had just come off the streets. Our contact said, "I'm really busy. I've got to take care of this boy, but I want to meet with you." One of the older boys said, "We'll take care of Sankar; you just enjoy the time with Pat." So they gave him some clothes and helped him. He took a bath and got cleaned up because he was dirty from being on the streets. Sankar ended up loving the place. I saw him a couple of weeks later and asked, "How are you doing, Sankar?" He said, "I love Jesus! I love Jesus!"

Sankar's family found out that he was alive. Someone had told them he was dead and that his organs had been sold in

India for transplants. They were devastated. When they found out he was alive, Sankar started communicating with them again. His family really wanted him back home and told him he could still go to school. So he asked the director of the home, "Can I go back home?"

The director told him, "If that's really what you want to do, you can go." Sankar decided it was. So the last I heard, Sankar was back in his village and doing well—going to school and serving the Lord.

Unfortunately, Raju is still on the streets. The last time I saw him, he was just ravaged by drugs. It is so grievous to see, but we continued to reach out. We're thankful for Sankar's rescue and the many others who have been saved. We thank God for all those He has brought across our path, and pray for more vulnerable kids to find refuge and hope in our children's homes.

On one of the trips to Nepal, our contact wanted me to visit a place called "tent city." It's a squatter's area where the people are very poor. I was able to go with a staff member from the ministry on my way to the airport. While we were walking through the area, I saw a young man about 12 years old who looked very sad. When I asked if I could take his picture, his face lit up and he smiled really big.

After taking his picture, the guy with me said, "Look at his feet!" I looked down and saw a big logging chain wrapped around his ankle. I was horrified—I had never seen a person in chains before. I asked why he was in chains. The neighbor man yelled at the young man; you could see the fear come over him. He tried his best to run into the shack he lived in. I demanded to know why he was in chains. The man told me he got into a lot of trouble and said, "His parents were afraid that he would run away."

Since I had to leave straight from there to catch my flight back to the U.S., I couldn't do anything more to help him, but I prayed for him for three months. I was also determined to go back and try to rescue him. When I closed my eyes, I saw that boy in chains; I couldn't get the image out of my mind.

Three months later, I went back to Nepal and talked to the director from one of the homes about helping me find him. He told me that after I had taken the picture, another neighbor had overheard the conversation and saw what was happening. He called the police. When the police came to check on the young man, they found out he had been kidnapped. He was being used as a slave. That night he was returned safely to his family!

I was so grateful to the Lord. Without even knowing what to do, God had used my being there and taking the picture of him to set him free! Sometimes we don't even know how God is using the things we do to impact the lives of others, but as we are obedient to Him, He will use our lives to set captives free!

# Chapter 8

# BANNED FROM CHINA

"By faith Abraham obeyed when he was called to go out to the place which he would receive as an inheritance. And he went out, not knowing where he was going. By faith he dwelt in the land of promise as in a foreign country, dwelling in tents with Isaac and Jacob, the heirs with him of the same promise; for he waited for the city which has foundations, whose builder and maker is God" (Hebrews 11:8-10 NKJV).

I don't think it's really even possible for me to express how disappointed I was the day I found out that I could not get a visa to go back into China. I truly went through a grieving stage, because at that time, I had been traveling in and out of China for over 21 years.

I really love the Chinese people, and I really love getting the Word of God to my brothers and sisters. There was a man from China who greatly impacted my life. His name is Pastor Allen Yuan. I met him when he was 89 years old. He had already spent 22 years in prison for his faith in Jesus Christ. He was actually in prison at the same time with Watchman Nee and Wang Ming Dao.

The first time I met him, I said, "What can we, as the

Church in America, do to help the Church in China?"

He said, "First of all, please pray for us. We have a lot of persecution; a lot of our leaders are in prison. But we are now 9% Christian. The government can't stop us now! The second thing we need is Bibles. We're desperate for Bibles."

Well, when an 89-year-old man, who has spent 22 years in prison, says, "We need Bibles!" you do what you can to help. I realized my response needed to be, "Lord, I want to do all I can to help him. If he's paid that price to serve You in his country, I feel like I need to help him by doing everything I can." So for years we carried Bibles to him and he was so grateful.

But I've gotten ahead of my story. I had actually gone to China with a young man from Sheridan, Wyoming. I called the Voice of the Martyrs ministry to ask for help. I told them, "I'm going to Beijing. Do you have a contact I could have in order to drop off some Bibles?" They said, "Yes, Pastor Allen," and they gave me his phone number.

We flew into Beijing with 320 Chinese Bibles in four suitcases. We also had some flannel graphs to help teach the stories of Jesus, many copies of the "JESUS" video, and a bunch of Gospel tracts in Chinese. I didn't realize until we were landing that it was the 13th anniversary of the June 4th Tiananmen Square Massacre. This is the event where the Chinese government attacked and killed pro-democracy students in mass while they were gathered for demonstrations in Beijing.

So, here we were—flying into Beijing—two Americans with lots of literature. I said, "Lord, we're dead ducks; we are so busted. Lord, we need a miracle today."

Thankfully, there were three flights that landed at the same time, so people were flooding into the Immigration and Customs area. I began to pray my way through, and waited to see how the Lord would open up some opportunities. I knew it would have to be God.

I told Tim, "Why don't you go through first?" He said, "Okay," and loaded his suitcases onto his cart. He also had a roller bag and backpack. When he got up by the X-ray machine, the Customs man said, "Sir, put your bags on the X-ray machine."

So he thought quickly and put his two hand-carried bags on the X-ray machine first. These bags only had his clothes in them, along with some tracts and the "JESUS" DVDs'. All of a sudden, the Customs man turned and looked away. Tim immediately took the cart holding his two big suitcases full of Bibles and went around the X-ray machine. Then he picked up his hand-carried bags and was out the door!

I said, "Okay, Lord, now how do I get through?"

At first, I saw a big group of European tourists. I thought, *I will go through with them*, but they were taking a very long time, so I decided that was not going to work.

Then I saw this tall Caucasian man, who was about 6' 8." I felt like the Lord said, "Get behind him." Naturally, I obeyed, and I began to follow him. By now, it was all bottlenecked by the X-ray machine and people were trying to get out of line to go around it.

As we got closer to the X-ray machine, I thought, *I'm going to get out of line and go around it, too!* But I felt the Holy Spirit say, "NO, stay behind this man!" As we got up to the X-ray machine, the man decided HE was going to get out of line and go around it. The Customs official told him, "Sir, put your bags on the X-ray machine!" He pointed at me and said, "Sir, you can go around." So I walked right around the X-ray machine and out the door with my suitcases full of Bibles and my carry-on luggage. I met up with Tim, got into a taxi, and went to the hotel.

After we checked into the hotel, we went to our room. I decided to call Pastor Allen. In China, the phones are bugged, so I didn't want to use the title of "pastor" on the phone. When I heard someone answer on the other end, I asked, "Is Allen there?"

They said, "Wait a minute."

Then, I heard a voice say very loudly, "I'm 89 years old and I'm hard of hearing! You have to yell into the telephone!"

I'm thinking, *I don't want to yell in the telephone. I'm in a Communist country, I've got all kinds of Bibles, and I don't want to yell!*

Voice of the Martyrs had told me about him. There was no way to email him to let him know we were coming. So he asked, "What's your name?"

"My name's Pat."

"Where are you from?"

"America."

"Where are you staying?"

I said, "The Yin Chang Hotel"

He said, "The WHAT?"

I said, "THE YIN CHANG HOTEL."

He wanted the address, the phone number, the room number … and then he asked, "Did you bring books?"

I thought, *Oh NO. Lord, they're going to storm our room any minute now. We're going to be arrested with these 320 Bibles and all this other stuff!*

I said, "I brought the books." Although, now I'm literally cringing as I'm thinking, *Oh, man. We are going to jail today.* Thankfully, God protected us, and about two hours later this little man who was only about five feet tall showed up.

He had come with his son. He had five kids. He was the pastor of a church in Beijing with around 1,500 people. Every year they would baptize 400 new Christians. He gave us a copy of his book, which was written by Brother Andrew's ministry, Open Doors. That's when I asked him, "What can we do to help you?"

It was so humbling to meet this man. Even though I didn't know his story at that time, I could just sense he was so full of the love of God and the humility of Jesus Christ. I was overwhelmed at his gratitude and simple request, as he said, "We're desperate for Bibles. Please bring us more Bibles!"

We carried the Bibles down to the lobby for him and then

loaded them into the taxi. They just took them to their house. He and his son were so grateful to get all these Bibles.

While we were traveling in China over the next couple of days, I began to read the book he had given me about his life. I read his testimony and was so convicted. He had spent 22 years in prison. At one point, when he had been in prison for 20 years, he was witnessing to an older man in his cell. The older man said, "Why don't you just renounce Jesus Christ? You can end all this pain and suffering today. You can go back to your wife and your five children tomorrow, if you just tell the communists you're sorry, you were wrong. You can end all this suffering and go home."

He said, "My suffering is so small compared to what Jesus went through on the cross."

When I read those words, I was so convicted. I thought, "Lord, forgive me for all the times I've complained about stupid, senseless stuff that doesn't matter. I sure haven't spent 22 years in prison for my faith."

Meeting this man and seeing the humility he walked in changed me. I said, "Lord, I want to do all I can to help him and the Christians in China." So we kept going back to bring in as many Bibles as we could.

One time, I had a team of 10 people with me and a total of 30 suitcases. Two guys got stopped, so we ended up giving him 26 suitcases of Bibles. When Pastor Allen and his wife came to our hotel to pick them up, the team was grateful for the opportunity to meet this man of God.

We all sat down on the floor and listened to Pastor Allen tell his story. I wanted to sit at his feet for weeks and listen to the wisdom God had given to him, especially after enduring so many trials. When the time came for them to leave, he tried to pick up the suitcases full of Bibles. His daughter said, "Dad, don't worry, we will get them." Even in his latter years, he wanted to serve people.

When I saw him the next time, I said, "Pastor Allen, do you remember us?" His memory had started to go and he replied, "I'm sorry, I don't remember," but his wife said, "You brought many suitcases filled with Bibles last time, yes? Many suitcases?" Immediately he said, "I remember you!"

It's really encouraging to me because I meet people who have heard Pastor Allen's testimony when I travel around the world. They have also been encouraged to stand up for Jesus in their countries and face persecution when it came.

One time, when I was visiting him, we had brought in a big load of Bibles. While we were talking with him and his wife, I said, "You know, Pastor Allen, your testimony has impacted believers all over the world and it has encouraged them to stand up for their faith." His wife told me they get many letters every day from people all over the world who thank him for his testimony.

The guy who was with me said, "Pastor Allen, just think about when you get to Heaven, the reward you're going to have!" At this time, he was 91 years old. He just closed his eyes, but after a few seconds, he got the biggest smile on his face. It was like he could see into Heaven and the reward before him.

I thought, "Wow, Lord! Thank you for letting him see that!" He died less than a year later. He's probably impacted my life more for the Gospel than anybody I know. Just seeing his life, hearing his testimony, and getting to know him had a great impact on me.

# Chapter 9

# ON THE ROAD TO BURMA

"Not to us, O LORD, not to us but to Your name be the
glory, because of Your love and faithfulness"
(Psalm 115:1 NIV).

My first time to Burma, which is now called Myanmar,
was 20 years ago. At that time, we didn't have a contact
person. I'd heard stories about how you're watched by the
government, but I wasn't sure exactly what to expect.

One day, we were walking around the downtown area, just praying. We turned down a side street and I saw a poster for a Christian movie. I asked some people nearby, "Are you Christians?"

They said, "No, no, but we know where a church is." So they directed us to a church, which was up on the fourth floor of an older British building. Just from appearances, there was no way you'd ever know there was a church up there.

We walked up the stairs and introduced ourselves to the pastor. We worked with this church for several years, providing them with Bibles every chance we had. We carried them in and also bought whatever we could from the Bible Society.

On one trip, we brought money for some missionaries to purchase more Bibles when they became available. One day, the man went to the Bible Society to purchase Bibles with the funds we had given him. While he was waiting in line, he overheard a Buddhist nun saying that she wanted to purchase a Bible, but couldn't afford one. He offered to give her one and she shared her story with him.

She explained that she was from Northern Burma. She had left her home to become a Buddhist nun. While she was riding the bus to Yangon, she sat next to a Christian lady who shared the Gospel with her. She was so excited to know more about this Jesus. Once she arrived in Yangon, she told another young nun that she was going to buy a Bible. The other nun asked if she would purchase a Bible for her as well. She also wanted to learn more about Jesus.

So this nun went to the Bible Society to purchase two Bibles, but she didn't have enough money to purchase even one! The missionary was able to give her the two Bibles; both she and her friend would have what they desired!

Our contacts in Burma have repeatedly requested Bibles. At one time, the Burmese government allowed the Bible Society to print 2,000 Burmese Bibles per year. If they printed more than 2,000, they had to omit the Virgin Birth because the Buddhists don't like Jesus being called God.

I knew the need for Bibles was great in Burma. So one time, when I was going in with a team of six men, I decided to do something we had never done before. We carried 1,000 Bibles in with us. We loaded 755 Bibles in our duffel bags and 245 Bibles in our hand-carried bags.

We were on an early flight from Bangkok, so we had to be at the airport at 6:00 a.m. It was a very heavy load of Bibles. We had to first pass through Immigration, and then on to Customs, where we were stopped.

The Customs people knew who I was. They had seen me bringing in Bibles many times before. In the past, when we had been stopped and they saw the Bibles, they still waved us through. This time, we got stopped by a military-looking Customs officer, who stepped up out of nowhere and said, "You can't bring Bibles into our country." He was very, very forceful, a real authoritarian. He said, "Today we're going to take all the Bibles away from you." And they started to confiscate all the Bibles.

I had heard stories about how they had burned Bibles a couple of years before that. Two thousand Bibles had come in from India and they burned them at the border. I was really frustrated thinking about this prospect, as I had just purchased them the day before from the Bible Society.

One of the guys on the team started talking with another Customs officer, who said, "Open your roller bag." Well, he opened his roller bag, but he had put his clothes on top—as I had instructed the team to do—and the Bibles underneath. The Customs officer never looked underneath the clothes. He said, "Close the bag up."

My friend then asked, "Could I give you a Bible?"

He said, "You know what? I'm a Buddhist, but my grandfather was a Christian. My grandfather loved Jesus and he loved his Bible. I'd really like to have a Bible, but I can't take it right now. They're watching me."

They held us for over three hours. Finally, I asked them, "Can my team go? They're really tired. We've been up since early this morning; this has already been a stressful day. Can they go to the hotel? I'll stay here as long as you need me to."

They said, "Yes, they can go."

So the team took the roller bags with the 245 Bibles they hadn't seen and left for the hotel. Now the authorities were packing up all 755 Bibles that they had confiscated and were preparing to take them away. It was right then that the Holy Spirit rose up in me.

When they said, "You have to sign this form," I said, "I'm not signing anything until you give me something in writing that says you're not going to destroy these Bibles. I've heard that you burn Bibles and I don't want you to burn any of these. I just bought them and I don't want you to destroy them."

A nicer Customs officer, who had come in after the militant officer left, said, "Sir, I promise you'll get these back on Monday." This was Saturday morning about noon.

I said, "Well, what guarantee do I have?"

He said, "I can't give you a piece of paper, but my name means 'Honest Friend,' and I promise that you will get them back on Monday!"

We shook hands, and I said, "In America, when you shake hands, it means you're giving your word. If I can't trust your word, I can't trust you as a man."

He said, "I promise you'll get these back on Monday."

I said okay and we shook hands; I signed the paperwork and went to the hotel. We prayed and committed the Bibles into the Lord's hands. During this episode, we called a pastor to help us. The military-looking Customs official threatened to have him arrested, so he sat quietly off to the side and left with the rest of the team.

The next morning, at nine o'clock, I received a phone call at the hotel. This was just Sunday, but I heard someone ask, "Can you come to the airport and bring your pastor friend with you? Please come at five o'clock today."

I said, "Okay."

Saturday and Sunday are holidays in Burma. For us to get an appointment at 5:00 on a Sunday afternoon was a true miracle.

We went to the airport at the time they asked us to be there, and Samuel, a man we've given a lot of Bibles to over the years, also came. Another man named Joseph met us there as well. I didn't know him, but a board member had met him on a previous trip.

Joseph arrived at the airport and he was literally shaking hands with everybody as he walked in the door. I had no idea what to expect or think. I've never seen anyone who knew so many people in my life! The military officer, who had taken the Bibles away from us, saw Joseph and left the building—I could tell he was mad. I kept wondering, "Lord, what are you doing?"

They took the four of us into this VIP room, where we met with four government leaders in Burma. The Minister of Religious Affairs, the Minister of Foreign Affairs, the head of Customs, and the man over the airport were there. All this happened on a Sunday afternoon at 5:00! I kept thinking, "Lord, this has got to be You at work!"

They said, "Now, Patrick, we like you and we appreciate you coming to our country, but you can't bring in 755 Bibles." They didn't know I had already taken in 245. They said, "You just can't bring in this many Bibles."

I asked, "Why not?"

They said, "You could bring in 1 or 2 or 5, but you can't

bring in almost 1,000 Bibles."

I asked again, "But why not?"

And they said, "You just can't do this."

So I said, "Well, where is it written that I can't?"

They replied, "Well, you just can't do this. This is too many Bibles."

I said, "God changed my life with His Word and His Spirit, and the best thing I know to do is to bring you the Word of God because God's given me hope and eternal life. Jesus has forgiven my sins and given me eternal life, and I want to share that with the Burmese people. So the best thing I know to do is to give you the Word of God. I love your people; I love coming to your country; this is one of my favorite places in the whole world. I love coming here because your people are honest, they tell the truth, and don't try to steal from me. I love coming here with my teams."

Finally, they said, "Okay, okay. I will tell you what, from now on, you contact Mr. Joseph. He'll get a piece of paper and you can bring in whatever you want into our country." Then they added, "Because we like you, we're going to give you all the Bibles back today."

I thought, *Only God could do that! Only God can change peoples' hearts!* So, they gave us back the Bibles. We gave them out to the contacts and 300 of them actually went to Buddhist monks who wanted them, so they could read the Word of God for themselves.

Five weeks later, four of us returned to Burma with 800

Bibles. We got stopped in Customs. The lady asked me, "What's in the bag?"

I said, "Books."

She said, "What kind of books?"

I said, "Spiritual books."

She said, "What kind of spiritual books?"

I said, "They're Bibles. I'm a Christian."

She walked over to me and said, "Patrick! You know you're not supposed to do this!" She knew me by name! She finished with, "Patrick, you know you're supposed to have a piece of paper."

I said, "Yes, Ma'am. I contacted Joseph two weeks ago. I sent him an email, but I haven't heard anything back. I didn't know what else to do. I had already bought the tickets."

She said, "Okay, okay, let them go. They're with Joseph; let them go."

Three weeks later, I came back again with three people. We had 600 Bibles. We walked into Customs and Joseph was standing there. I said, "Joseph, did you bring the piece of paper?"

He said, "I'm your piece of paper!"

He literally walked over, shook hands with all these people and walked us right through Customs.

I went back a couple of months later. This time, we had 1,400 Bibles. It was the biggest load we had ever carried into Burma. The bags all had an "X" marked on them with chalk, which means they're supposed to be checked in at Customs, but we walked right through.

When I went to see Joseph, I said, "Joseph, I didn't see you at the airport today."

He said, "Sorry, I got busy. So I called Customs and told them, "Patrick and his team are coming today. Let him through." And that's exactly what they did ... we walked right through.

I learned you can never underestimate God's favor. The Word is clear ... we have favor with God ... and we have favor with man!

# Chapter 10

# MIRACLE IN A BAG

"As evening approached, the disciples came to him and said, 'This is a remote place, and it's already getting late. Send the crowds away, so they can go to the villages and buy themselves some food.' Jesus replied, 'They do not need to go away. You give them something to eat.' 'We have only five loaves of bread and two fish,' they answered. 'Bring them here to me,' he said. And he directed the people to sit down on the grass. Taking the five loaves and the two fish and looking up to heaven, he gave thanks and broke the loaves. Then he gave them to the people. They all ate and were satisfied, and the disciples picked up twelve basketfuls of broken pieces that were left over" (Matthew 14:15-20 NIV).

After Cyclone Nargis, we carried many supplies and funds into Burma to help the people. We got stopped in Customs and the lady asked, "What's in the bag?"

I said, "Seeds and clothes."

She said, "Okay, go through. Have a nice day."

Joseph met us a little while later. I said, "Joseph, we got right through!" He said, "I know. I called and told them you had eight duffel bags with seeds and clothes in them."

We were able to travel down to the delta area and give

out many supplies. We were down to just two duffel bags full of clothes when we came to the last village. There were 250 families who desperately needed clothing. We started to pull clothes out of the bags to give them what we had left. All the while I was thinking, "Lord, there's no way there's going to be enough clothes here to take care of 250 families."

As I continued to pull clothes from the bag, it was like they were multiplying right in front of my eyes. I kept reaching in and pulling them out—reaching in and pulling them out. I thought, "Lord, the bag is not even going down. It's not going down!" It was beyond amazing. This was truly a miracle, just like when Jesus fed the five thousand with just five loaves of bread and two fish.

Everybody had clothes and we still had another duffel bag we hadn't even opened yet. So we began to give out handfuls of clothes to each person. God was multiplying it right in front of our eyes. The key was for us to be in a place where we truly needed Him to move, where there was no other option for their provision. Because our only hope was in God's provision, and we had to depend on Him, it allowed us to really see Him at work.

It's amazing how God does it, how He opens doors in response to His children's prayers. We just keep praying, "God, give us the right connections in the right places, so we can get stuff done quickly. There isn't a lot of time to try to go out and build relationships with everybody." I've seen the faithfulness of God time and time again. It's been exciting to watch Him at work and to see how He opens doors and touches peoples' hearts. It's truly been amazing.

The lessons God has taught me through my Bible smuggling experiences over the years can really be summed up in this: You've got to be obedient. When God says to do something, just do it! Don't ask questions, just do it! It may not always make sense. And we may not even understand what He's doing right at that moment, but when we obey, God will always work out all the rest!

When I first went into the country of Burma, it was with a few Bibles. When I first went into China, it was with twenty Bibles. But as my faith grew, I was able to believe the Lord for hundreds, even thousands of Bibles. The need is so great. My faith, which was so small when I first started out, still grows when I witness what the Lord can do.

I've learned that it's repetition. I keep going back and I'm committed to working with the people. I keep saying, "We're here to serve. What do you need?" Today, we have delivered over 60,000 Bibles to Burma alone. I can't say it enough, "To God be the glory!"

# Chapter 11

# THE MOST RADICAL ISLAMIC COUNTRY

"For we do not preach ourselves but Christ Jesus as Lord, and ourselves as your bond-servants for Jesus' sake. For God, who said, 'Light shall shine out of darkness,' is the One who has shone in our hearts to give the Light of the knowledge of the glory of God in the face of Christ" (2 Corinthians 4:5-6 NASB).

It was my first trip to Iran and I had 80 Farsi New Testaments packed in my luggage. I was meeting the team in Turkey before traveling into this strict Islamic country. I checked in my suitcases and then reality hit me. I thought, *What did I just do? I'm traveling to the most radical Islamic country in the world and I have Bibles in my bag.* It's not that we don't have people praying for us because we do, but I immediately called one of our board members and asked him to contact the other members to pray.

My aunt had married an Iranian man many years before and I enjoyed spending time with my uncle. I was fascinated by the fact that he was from Iran and I believe God used him to put a seed of interest in my heart for the country of Persia. Now, years later, as I approached Tehran my heart was excited, but I was also worried about what would happen if they found Bibles in my luggage.

We arrived in Tehran at 4:00 a.m. The women were covered from head to toe in black. You could feel the oppression in the air, and the underlying fear was evident. We approached the Immigration counter and presented our passports. The young man finished processing our visas and said, "We need to fingerprint you because you are Americans. Come with me, I love Americans!" I thought, *This is so different from what I've seen in the media.*

After being fingerprinted, he told us to go through Customs. I peered over the balcony that overlooked the Customs area. I saw the two X-ray machines and the carousel with our suitcases sitting on the floor. I noticed there were no Customs agents. When you're carrying Bibles into closed countries and there are no Customs agents, it's a good thing!

I thought, *I need to try and get through quickly.*

By the time we reached the X-ray machine, a man had come out of nowhere. He barked at me with a stern voice, "Put your suitcases on the X-ray machine." My heart was pounding. Now the question was no longer "if" they find the Bibles, but what they would do to me as a result. Would they cut off my head ... or take me out back and shoot me?

I lifted the bags onto the X-ray machine. The Customs official asked, "Are you tourists?"

We said, "Yes."

He barked back with an intimidating voice, "Where are you from?"

I said, "We're Americans."

His countenance immediately softened. He asked with gentleness in his tone, "You're from America? I *love* America! Take your suitcases off the X-ray machine. You can go right through. You're *Americans!*"

I exhaled a sigh of relief. It's at moments like this that you can't help but realize that God truly is the ruler over all the nations of the Earth!

Everywhere we went, when people found out we were Americans, they went crazy. I have never felt as welcomed in any other country that I have traveled to for the Lord. The people we met were wonderful, and they absolutely loved Americans!

It is reported that there are over one million Christians in Iran today.[1]  I've heard that 80% of the people who come to faith in Jesus Christ have had a dream or a vision from Jesus.

Our team visited a tourist site, and while we were there, we met a group of young men on a school tour. When they found out we were Americans, they went crazy, too—shaking our hands and hugging us! Camera phones came out from everywhere! It was like we were celebrities with the paparazzi … they desperately wanted our pictures.

Afterwards, both our groups moved on to different sites, but one of our members stayed back. When no one was looking, a young man from the school tour ran back and asked him, "The Messiah—is He dead or alive?"

He replied, "Jesus died on the cross and rose again on the third day. Jesus is alive!"

The young man replied, "He's alive?!"

The team member said, "Yes, He's alive!"

Elated, the young man said, "Thank you, thank you!" and ran out.

On the day we were traveling from Mashhad to Shiraz, we entered the airport and were required to put our suitcases through the X-ray machine. My suitcases were mixed in with the rest of our group's luggage. As we walked through the metal detector, I was called over by the security guard. He singled me out and asked me to open my suitcases. The other team members waited off to the side, praying for God's intervention.

I opened the two suitcases. My heart was beating at what seemed to be a hundred miles an hour—yet at the same time it felt like it had stopped. The security guard saw the Farsi Bibles. He reached into the suitcase and pulled one of them out. He slowly opened it and started to read it. He was reading the verses of Scripture as though he was interested in the contents.

He put it back into the bag and then took out another one. (They were all exactly the same.) He studied it very closely, reading the verses. Then, he put that one back in and took out a third book. Our tour guide was standing next to him. He asked him, "Are you looking for a gun in there?"

The security guard said, "What?"

The tour guide asked again, "Are you looking for a gun?" Then he began to laugh.

The security guard looked puzzled for a moment, but then he said, "Close your bags; you can go."

Once again I witnessed the faithfulness of God!

When we reached our hotel safely, I began to think about the amazing thing that had just happened. It also occurred to me that the tour guide had seen all the Bibles in my bag. This meant he knew the real reason I was in Iran.

I went to his room that night and asked him if I could talk with him. He invited me in. I began to share the Gospel, telling him my testimony. Then he opened up his heart and told me the story of his life. I prayed for God to reveal the Truth to him, and before leaving, I presented him with a Farsi Bible. He said, "Thank you; I promise you, I will read this book every day!"

The day before we left, our whole team was sad we would be leaving so soon. I told our tour guide I had never felt so welcomed in any country of the world—the people were so hospitable. I wished more Americans could visit his country to see its beauty and meet the people. I told him I was having a hard time leaving because I felt like I was leaving a part of me in his country. He thanked me and walked away. A few minutes later he returned with tears in his eyes; he had been crying. I thought to myself, he is supposed to be my mortal enemy, but the Holy Spirit is drawing him and instead we have become good friends! We returned home to the U.S., thankful to God for another trip where He was glorified.

But time passes quickly, and soon it was time for me to take my second trip to Iran. This trip was a lot more adventurous. I thought since God had gotten me through with 80 Bibles without any major incidents, this time I should take more— not a hundred or a hundred fifty more, but two hundred.

Unfortunately, this time I was stopped in Customs at 2:30 in the morning. When they saw the Bibles go through the X-ray machine, they immediately wanted me to open my bags. I don't know what surprised them most: seeing the Bibles, or the large quantity of them! We were sent all over the airport.

Finally, a head Customs officer came and reported that they needed to confiscate the books and read them to make sure they were the Word of God. I thought, *Are you kidding? Like I would object to them actually reading the Bible?* I told them it was okay if they wanted to read them. I knew God could touch their hearts while they read His Word.

Our tour guide led me around to meet the appropriate officials. Finally, we were taken into a room, where the man in charge of this area was directed to confiscate the Bibles in my suitcases. The tour guide asked if we could give him a Bible. Of course I agreed. When I handed it to him, his face immediately lit up and he quickly hid it out of sight. Then he did his job and confiscated the rest of them.

They failed to see the 20 Bibles that were still left in my carry-on baggage; so for the next seven days I gave them out to various people, including one to a team member for her to give out. On our last day, we were in the market and a university student approached her. He spoke very good English and offered to help her find the things she was looking for. He shared about the oppression in the country and how he needed to get out, to build a life somewhere else and know freedom. He said, "There is no future for me in this country; there is no hope!" She shared the Gospel with him and gave him the Farsi Bible. His face lit up and he said, "I now have a reason to live!"

On that same day, I wandered around the market, praying and asking God to show me who I was supposed to give the few remaining Bibles to. I walked by a university student who invited me into his shop to purchase a Persian carpet. I told him I was leaving the next day and didn't have much money left. He asked me to join him for a cup of tea. I followed him into the shop and sat down while he poured us some tea.

We talked for a while. I was able to share the Gospel with him. He was very receptive. Before I left, I presented him with a Farsi Bible. His face lit up. He said, "I can't believe I have the Word of God now; I have the Truth! Please be careful giving these out, but I have the Truth now!" and he started to cry. He was so grateful to get the Truth of Jesus Christ.

In many places around the world, we find people very hungry for the Truth. When presented with a Bible, tears fill their eyes, especially when they realize Jesus is the Truth.

We've partnered with the Iranian Christians in Turkey, and they report that out of 1,000 Iranians, only 3 or 4 of them are closed to the Gospel. There is such a tremendous harvest field in Iran!

A man we worked with in Iran told us, "Nobody believes Islam anymore in this country. The government has destroyed this religion in our eyes!"

# Chapter 12

# POLICE INTERFERENCE

"Therefore, my dear brothers and sisters, stand firm. Let nothing move you. Always give yourselves fully to the work of the Lord, because you know that your labor in the Lord is not in vain" (1 Corinthians 15:58 NIV).

In 1988, there was a great outpouring of the Holy Spirit on the Vietnamese Church. Many believers were gathered together in prayer when they experienced a move of the Holy Spirit similar to the disciples on the Day of Pentecost. They didn't understand what was happening to them until they read the Book of Acts. Several churches were birthed from this outpouring and the church leaders invited us to come. They were hungry for God's Word.

Some of these leaders felt forgotten by the global Body of Christ. We assured them that millions of Christians from all over the world were praying for them. Tears welled up in their eyes; they were so grateful!

My first trip to Vietnam was in 1992. At that time, the country was just beginning to open its doors to the outside world. It was really exciting because I didn't know what to expect.

My friend, Mark, and I flew in with a load of Gospel literature in the Vietnamese language. We were nervous as we approached the Customs hall. The people were all bunched together in this small room. The bags were lifted off the floor. Then, they were loaded onto carts and wheeled past the Customs officers.

I have discovered that regardless of how many years I've traveled, or how many times I've done this, going through Customs always has an opportunity to present problems. This time was no exception. My heart began to race as a lady approached us. She wanted to see our paperwork.

She was dressed in the traditional Vietnamese outfit—white flowing pants, covered by a long sky blue blouse that reached to the floor. Her warm smile welcomed us to Vietnam. She walked alongside us, escorting us past the guards and then out of the room. The other passengers were made to wait as the guards sifted through their belongings. We were relieved, knowing again that truly God's grace was with us as He had opened the way before us!

One day, we met a guy we felt might be open to the Gospel, so we asked if we could buy him lunch. He agreed, telling us he knew a very good restaurant along the street. We were surprised and shocked when we arrived at a restaurant that was barbequing dogs! The first dog was about half consumed, while the other full-sized dog was being cooked on a rotisserie.

Wisely, Mark said he was fasting that day, so I ordered noodles and vegetables. They brought me a bowl of noodles and vegetables with dog meat on top. I ate a piece of the dog meat. The taste itself wasn't so bad, sweet and tender. The problem was just in knowing what I was eating!

Mark and I decided to travel from Saigon to Hanoi by road. It would have been much faster by airplane, but we wanted to see the country and distribute Gospel tracts along the way. The trip ended up taking 57 hours of broken travel. We rode public buses and stopped in the small town of Lang Co along the ocean. It was beautiful, and we even had the beach to ourselves for miles. The only drawback was food; we only had ramen noodles and eggs.

It was a restful few days, swimming in the ocean and having devotions on the beach. I remember the long walks on the beach—talking to the Lord, singing and worshipping

Him. It was a sweet time of fellowship and I enjoyed His presence. Then it was time to continue our trip up North.

We also spent a few days in Hue, and I distinctly remember something that happened one night while we were in the hotel. Mark was in the bathroom when there was a knock at the door. It was the manager and he had a beautiful woman with him. He offered for her to give me a massage. I told him, "No, we're not interested," so they left.

They returned about 30 minutes later and Mark answered the door. The manager asked if Mark wanted her for the night, to which he quickly replied, "No, please leave us alone." This was my first brush with human trafficking. I was disgusted and saddened to see such a lack of respect toward women.

Mark and I worked during the day, rolling Gospel tracts in small plastic bags and securing them with rubber bands. We would wait until dark, and then one of us would sit by the window to toss tracts out of the bus, while the other watched to make sure no one was looking. We took turns whenever one of us became tired.

In the early '90s, the most common mode of transportation in Vietnam was the bicycle. There were many villages along this highway, so we knew people would ride their bicycles and find the tracts.

It was obvious when we crossed from South to North Viet nam—the North was much poorer. The well-maintained, two-lane highway in the South became almost non-existent in places because sand covered more than one lane. At certain points, it seemed we were driving through the sand because the road was so hard to see.

Mark and I stayed up all night, switching back and forth to finish distributing the tracts on the last leg of our trip. The oppression increased, and you could sense the underlying fear as we approached the capital. It was amazing—right as I finished throwing the last tract, we entered the city. God's timing was perfect; the sun was just beginning to rise as we pulled into Hanoi!

We were elated, knowing that within hours the tracts would be picked up by people who were riding their bikes along the highway. We prayed that many people would read the tracts, repent of their sins, and put their faith in Christ.

After several years of delivering Bibles and teaching materials to help strengthen the Vietnamese and tribal Church, we asked what more we could do to help them. I was on a team with two other Americans and we had returned to help encourage the Church in Saigon. After delivering supplies to our contacts, they asked us if we would be willing to teach on spiritual warfare and prayer. We agreed, and they were very excited.

We were staying in a guesthouse, which was quite large. The owner had informed us that she was a Christian. We invited the believers to come to the guesthouse and 38 Christians from three different denominational groups showed up. We had planned to teach for three days as they had requested, but one of the pastors announced he had a problem on the first morning. He did not want to meet in these conditions. He wanted their group to have a separate meeting away from everyone else. We had felt uneasy with this pastor from the beginning.

Our desire was to see the Christians from different denominations come together, so they could work together. We explained this to the pastor and told him we could not do separate meetings. He left upset. Less than ten minutes later, the police showed up.

I was actually teaching about our authority as believers in Jesus Christ when they arrived, and I was using a policeman as an example. While I was sharing, the two people with me said, "Pat! There's a policeman at the door right now!"

The police came in and started to harass everyone. The Vietnamese Christians quickly tried to hide their Bibles underneath the rug and couch because they were afraid the police would take them. The Bibles not hidden fast enough were confiscated, along with the worship leader's guitar and tambourines. Then they arrested all 38 believers. We asked some of them if they were afraid and they said they weren't. One older lady said, "This happens almost every time I go to a house church meeting." It was her third arrest in just a few months.

More police arrived and herded the group of Vietnamese Christians two blocks down the street to a small local police station, where they were held for two hours. During this time, the believers worshipped and prayed together, shared testimonies, and witnessed to the police. They asked them, "Why are we being arrested? We are not drug dealers, prostitutes, murderers, or thieves."

The police replied, "We don't know why we are arresting you; you are good people, law-abiding citizens. This is our job. We have to do this." The police were going to fine them about two dollars each, but the believers said it was too much, so the police lowered the price to one dollar each. The Christians rejoiced because they knew they had done nothing wrong!

Then the police brought a van to the front of the guesthouse and told the three of us to get in. When you check into a hotel or guesthouse in Vietnam, they automatically take your passport to fill out a police report and give it back to you when you check out; so the police already had our passports. When we arrived at the police station, we were told to sit down and wait.

One thing I have learned about traveling in Communist countries is that they like to use time as a form of control— making people wait long periods with no communication. It's also a silent method of trying to produce fear in those who are waiting.

The building was old and run down. There was very little furniture in the room and we were made to wait on a bench for about two hours. At this point, we were very hungry, so we gave them some money and asked for food. They brought back three sandwiches that contained slices of raw pork fat, which were positioned between two buttered pieces of bread. Needless to say, we didn't eat them.

A young man, who spoke very good English, was also there and interpreted for us. He asked us what had happened, so we explained. Since we had been waiting for several hours, we asked him what the problem was. He insisted there was no problem and we would be released in a short time. He said we had done nothing wrong.

Now, the lady who owned the guesthouse was at the police station. She played the part of a chameleon quite well. She would laugh and joke with the police in the room, then come out and tell us we had gotten her into trouble and cry. She would say things we knew weren't true and put on a sad face, but immediately change when she went back in with the police.

After about six hours of waiting, they said we could go back to the guesthouse, but we couldn't leave it. Since they had our passports, we couldn't go anywhere anyway.

The next day, we were taken back to the police station where they showed us a little book listing the penalties for breaking the laws in Vietnam. The booklet said the lowest penalty was two hundred dollars and the highest penalty was deportation. We were told that we would be fined two hundred dollars each because we had come into the country on tourist visas, but were doing religious work instead.

I asked, "If I came as a businessman on a business visa, but did tourist activities, would I be fined?" They insisted that

I would. We felt this was a real injustice as we were only trying to help the believers.

I tried to reach out to several people from the American Embassy in Bangkok. At this point, the United States did not have any diplomatic relations with Vietnam and there wasn't a U.S. Embassy in the country. The man I talked to from the U.S. Embassy in Bangkok said, "Just pay the fine and go!" Since we were on limited funds, we insisted on being deported, to which they replied, "No, it's not that serious!" It was obvious that all they wanted was to get as much money from us as possible.

Vietnam is a police state and everything is closely monitored. I realized later that all the cyclo drivers are informants and the security guards in larger hotels are undercover police. Even the taxi drivers report your whereabouts to the police. Everywhere we went, spies followed us, watching our every move. We tried to move to a different guesthouse, but were unable to do so without our passports.

After three days, I went back to the police station and tried again to negotiate a lower fine, but they refused. They moved the issue from the local police station to a much larger central police station.

By the sixth day, I felt we needed to get a resolution. I went to the police station and said, "First of all, you've had our passports for more than five days. You've broken international law because my passport is not really my passport; it's the property of the U.S. Government. According to U.S. law, if you have my passport for more than five days, you have to contact my embassy. It becomes an international issue because you have us under house arrest and we can't go anywhere."

They talked among themselves for a few minutes and then returned our passports. They told us we were still required to pay the fine, but now it would be split between several more people.

In the hallway, I saw the head policeman from the small local station we were taken to in the beginning. He had been very difficult to work with, but I felt impressed by the Lord to shake his hand and thank him. So I went over and said, "I just want to thank you very much. I'll be praying for you. God bless you."

He said, "No, I want to thank you." I believe he knew we were unjustly treated and the fine was unreasonable. I also think he saw that we tried to stand up for what was right as Christians, even though it would have been more convenient to back down.

After talking with this man, we went back into the room with the police. We paid the fine, but told them we would much rather help the people by spending it at their markets, hotels, and restaurants.

It was difficult for me, as an American, to see how Christians in many countries of the world have no rights. The laws change daily, and what's legal today, is illegal tomorrow. This incident caused me to pray more for Christians in closed countries and do all I can to help them. They are learning to trust God and serve Him in a hostile environment. I believe we need to learn from their example and have a determination in our hearts to serve the Lord, regardless of what happens in our country!

That wasn't our only time to go to Vietnam. They had been asking us to come and teach them for years, so we planned a trip with that purpose. Believers came from all over and secretly met at a designated safe house where the meetings would take place.

Each day, someone picked me up by motorcycle. To avoid attention, I wore a jacket and baseball cap to cover my light-colored skin and hair. The driver would take me around Saigon for about thirty minutes—down back alleys and in crazy patterns—before dropping me at the safe house. He would literally drive straight inside the house, let me off in the hallway, and leave. Then I would quickly run upstairs to teach, making sure that I didn't attract the attention of someone passing by.

At the end of the day, the motorcycle would pull back into the hallway, pick me up, and drive in all these different directions before bringing me back to my hotel. This went on for several days.

The teaching sessions lasted 8 hours each day because the believers were that hungry to learn! The schedule was exhausting, but they were so gracious and teachable. They kept bringing me cold drinks, and asking, "Are you okay?

Can you teach a little longer?"

They wrote down everything I said, and when I finished, they asked question after question because they were so eager to learn more. Immediately they put into practice what they were taught. They were very humble and grateful, always thanking me afterwards. It was incredible to see the Holy Spirit moving among these believers and to witness their intense desire for God.

We have been carrying Bibles into Vietnam for over 20 years now, but the need is still tremendous. God is really pouring out His Spirit on the tribal people. They helped the CIA during the Vietnam War, and as a result, are hated by the Communists. They often face persecution at the hands of the government, even to the point of having to bury their Bibles when the Communist leaders come to their villages. God has blessed our teams as they cross the borders with His Word. By His grace, we have been able to help supply many Scriptures to these people in their native dialects.

The believers have also requested songbooks in their language. We found some and brought the songbooks to them. When they received them, they started to cry, saying, "We can worship God with all our 'liver' now!" We wondered, "What on Earth does that mean?" But we learned that they see the center of their being as their liver and not their heart. So what they were really saying is that they could worship God with all of their being.

On another trip, we were given 500 Bibles to take to a

remote tribal group. There were thousands of Christians in this group and they had never had Bibles in their own dialect. Our team that was carrying the first load of these Bibles crossed the border successfully and delivered a large load to our contact. The pastor was so excited; he had never seen the Bible in this dialect before.

I had the last load of these Bibles and flew into Vietnam. After clearing Immigration, I proceeded to Customs, where I had to put the duffel bags on an X-ray machine. The lady watching the screen saw the Bibles. I was praying that everything would make it through safely.

Then the Customs officer called me over and told me to open the duffel bags. I said, "Okay," and started to lift the bags off the machine onto my cart, praying the whole time.

Again she said, "Sir, come over here and open your bags!"

I said, "Okay," but I kept loading the bags onto the cart, still praying and asking for the Lord's intervention.

Then she said, "Sir, come over here *now* and open your bags!"

I had just finished loading all the bags and made my way over to her desk. She said, "Ahh, never mind, go ahead and go. Have a nice day!"

Once again, God's faithfulness and protection was demonstrated before my eyes!

The man we have worked overseas with for years has many churches among the tribal Christians. Every time we deliver a large load of Bibles, he is very grateful. On one trip we delivered over 1,000 Bibles. There were nine on the team and not one person was stopped. I had called him that morning to tell him that I was coming with a team and we would arrive later that night.

After clearing Customs, we walked out of the airport and there was our contact with his sweet wife. They were surprised to see nine people with so many duffel bags. He quickly went to work, arranging for more vehicles to take us to the safe house. Upon arrival, many of his workers came to help us unload these bags that were full of Bibles. Sometimes, these bags are so heavy that it takes three Asian men to lift one of them, as they weigh more than the person carrying them.

After all the books were unloaded, they stood there in disbelief at so many copies of God's precious Word. They were very grateful! Our contact shared how just two days before, the Christians had requested more Bibles. He told them, "We need to pray. I don't know when the next team is coming."

The previous day he had been in another area of his country and the believers there said, "Pastor, we need more Bibles." He replied, "I don't know when they are coming; we need to pray." That night they prayed, asking God for more Bibles. He returned home late that night.

It was the next morning when I called to say we were coming! He thought we would have one or two people with about 200 Bibles; instead, we had more than 1,000!

With joy he exclaimed, "God heard our prayer! God heard

our prayer! Can you bring us 10,000 more?!"

When I hear these requests, I cannot help but want to keep supplying more Bibles. "I ask You, Lord, can we bring them 10,000 more? Only by faith, Lord, only by faith!"

# Chapter 13

# CUBA—AN ILLEGAL LAND

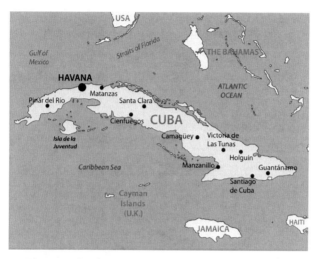

"The Lord reigns; let the earth rejoice; Let the multitude of isles be glad!" (Psalm 97:1 NKJV).

Cuba is one of those countries that people often ask, "Isn't it illegal to go there?" I have been traveling to Cuba for over 20 years, bringing Bibles and support to the pastors there. It is true, according to U.S. law we are not supposed to travel to Cuba because we have trade sanctions against the country.

In Matthew 28:18-20, it says, "And Jesus came and spoke to them, saying, 'All authority has been given to Me in heaven and earth. Go therefore and make disciples of all the nations, baptizing them in the name of the Father and of the Son and of the Holy Spirit, teaching them to observe all things that I have commanded you; and lo, I am with you always, even to the end of the age.'"

Jesus gave us the Great Commission. He didn't tell us to just go to the countries where they welcome you with open arms, or where your government has good relationships. I believe we are to obey the laws of the land where we live or travel to visit, but if those laws conflict with God's laws, His are higher and need to be obeyed regardless of what the government or religious leaders say.

On my first trip to Cuba, I was traveling alone from Jamaica with 125 Bibles. I wanted to go to Cuba to see what I could do because I knew the people were very hungry for the Word of God and needed help. Flying into Cuba with 125 Bibles was risky business. At Customs, they wanted to see what was in my bags, so I opened them. They looked through the contents, and then asked, "Do you have Bibles?"

I said, "Yes."

They asked, "How many do you have?"

I replied, "Oh, probably a hundred and some."

They snapped, "What?! You can't bring 100 Bibles in here!"

I asked, "Why not?"

They said, "Well, you're just not allowed to."

I asked again, "Why not? I flew in from Jamaica today and even paid overweight charges to carry all these books in.

There's nothing in Jamaica that says I can't bring Bibles to your country. There's nothing written in your Customs regulations. There's no sign in your Customs hall or Immigration that says a person can't bring Bibles into this country. Where is it written that one can't bring in Bibles?"

He hedged, "Well, you just can't bring in 100 or more Bibles into our country! Maybe two or three or five at the most, but you can't bring 100 Bibles in here!" Then, they began to confiscate them.

I said, "Sir, I would never dream of bringing drugs or pornography into your country, but I bring you the Bibles because I know it is the Truth. The Truth has set me free. God used His Word and His Spirit to show me the Truth, to set me free, and to save me from my sins. I bring you hope because Jesus has given me hope. I have come to bring this hope to your country. Therefore, you can do whatever you want, but I have done my job. I am trusting God."

It was very discouraging because I thought, *What's going to happen now? Will those Bibles be burned? Will they be destroyed?*

For the next three days I was on a package tour. The tour guide, Juan, was a very nice guy and open to the Gospel. After befriending Juan and sharing Christ with him, I confided to him that I had come to his country with 125 Bibles. I told him how Customs had confiscated them and that I was really concerned the Bibles would be burned.

He said, "Patrick, don't worry. Those Bibles will not be

burned. They will be sold on the black market because the Word of God is too valuable. Customs officials can get money for them."

In some ways, as strange as it may seem, I was somewhat relieved. My thought was, *If we can get the Bibles into a country, then they have that many more than they did the day before, so its God's job to get them through Customs.*

I learned years ago that my job is to carry them in. Then I have to trust God to get them through. Many times He gets us through. Sometimes we are stopped, which provides an opportunity to share the Gospel with the Customs agents. We pray that we are a testimony for Jesus everywhere we go.

During this same trip to Cuba, I decided to go on a half-day package tour, which gave me an opportunity to see the old city of Havana. It was also going to provide a little time for some relaxation. The tour gave us a half-hour break for lunch. We were told that we could browse the streets of old Havana, have lunch, and then the tour guide would pick us back up to finish the tour.

I stepped off the bus, wondering where I would go and what I would do. I prayed for the Lord to direct my steps and to use me for His glory. As I walked down the street, I saw a shop and felt impressed by the Lord to go in. Right inside the door, a young man was sitting there reading the New Testament. I said to him, "Excuse me. Are you a Christian?"

He replied, "No, but my wife is. I want to become a Christian, but I don't know how. You know, my wife is a very godly woman. She loves God. I watch her life, and I see Jesus in her life."

I began to talk with him and share the Gospel. Then, I prayed with him for salvation. I gave him some Gospel tracts. Before I left the shop, he was already sharing the Gospel tracts with the other workers in the shop!

On another trip to Cuba, I was having a morning quiet time with the Lord when He opened an opportunity in my hotel room. I was reading my Bible and listening to some worship tapes when I heard a knock at my door. It was the cleaning lady, Inez.

I tried to share the Gospel with her, but my Spanish is very limited. She seemed very receptive, so I went to find two of the women from my team. One of them, Elsa, spoke fluent Spanish and she helped me share the Gospel and lead Inez to Christ. Inez wanted to repent of her sins and put her faith and trust in Jesus. After we prayed with her for salvation, she thanked us and went back to her cleaning. I went back to my quiet time.

About twenty minutes later, Inez knocked on my door again. She had brought her friend, another cleaning woman. She said, "This lady also wants to become a Christian!" I quickly ran to get Elsa to help translate and we shared the Gospel with this friend, who also received the Lord.

It was really exciting, and we were so happy and thankful to the Lord. They left, and again I went back to my quiet time. It wasn't 10 minutes later when Inez knocked once more and she had a young man with her this time. Elsa helped translate again. He told us that he needed Bibles. He said his uncle was the pastor of a large congregation at a Baptist Church, but only a few of the people had Bibles. He shared that his uncle was very evangelistic.

He added, "When we go to a Bible study in the home groups, we have only one Bible for fifteen, twenty or twenty-five people in the room. We pass that Bible around so people can read from it."

We had already given most of our Spanish Bibles to a pastor, who we later discovered worked with the government-controlled church. I felt convicted and wished I had kept those Bibles to give to this young man. They needed many more Bibles for their congregation and work among the unsaved.

I gave him the five we had left and he was very, very grateful. On the next couple of trips we made to Cuba, we delivered more and more Bibles for his uncle's congregation.

Having various pastors ask us to bring in Bibles was a common occurrence. One of these pastors was a man named Carlos. My friend, Karl, and I were down in the streets of old Havana one day passing out Gospel tracts. We happened to run into a young man named Henry. He said he wanted us to meet his friend, Carlos, a pastor. The two men were very close and called each other "brother."

At that time, Carlos' congregation was meeting in his apartment, where he lived with his wife and four children. We attended the service; it was amazing. We counted 91 people—

all packed into that little apartment. People were standing in the kitchen, bathroom, in front of the open door, and even on the steps that led up to the small front porch. They were crammed together in that little apartment to hear the Word of God. We were blessed to be there and have since built a relationship with Pastor Carlos. He continues to be one of our contacts in Cuba.

About six months after meeting Carlos, some friends and I went back into Cuba with another load of Bibles. However, we couldn't find Carlos' church. Fortunately, some people led us to his new apartment, which was about a block away. It was much larger, and now, this was his new church. There were now 231 people packed in this house church. People were even standing outside the doors and windows to hear the Word of God. They were grateful to receive the 15 Bibles we had.

In Cuba, the government does not allow any new churches. The congregations must meet in existing church buildings. If any new churches spring up, they have to be in houses or storefronts. Even in those circumstances, they can be shut down at any time. Often they are discovered by undercover police who attend these services. The larger churches are watched by the police. They come to the services to take note of what the pastor is saying and see who is in attendance. But, in spite of the controls, God is really working. Foreigners are not permitted to preach in the churches, but they can bring greetings and mix a short devotion in their greeting.

On one specific trip, we were flying to Cuba from Jamaica. We had 550 hardcover Spanish Bibles with us. We had packed our bags that morning. In addition to the Bibles, we were bringing in flannel graphs, medical supplies, and clothing that people had donated for the kids and children in the orphanages. As we were passing through Customs, we were really praying. One of the guys had hidden Gospel tracts under his shirt.

I was first through the security check point and had to put my carry-on bag through the X-ray machine. There were ten Spanish Bibles in that bag. The woman could see something on the X-ray screen, so she asked me to open my bag. When she saw the Spanish Bibles, she told me to close up my bag and move on.

On my previous trips to Cuba, I had never seen anyone actually having their body searched. This time, the Customs agents were searching every person's body as they came through Immigration. I was concerned. As they patted me down, I thought, *What about that guy with the tracts hidden under his shirt?* It was too late to send him to the restroom to take them out.

He wasn't very far behind me, and as the Customs agent asked to search his body, we all lifted up a quick prayer for God's help. The Customs agent saw the Gospel tracts, looked at them, apologized, and let him go!

After the woman had seen the ten Bibles in my carry-on

bag, she called on a walkie-talkie to a Customs official in the area where suitcases come off the conveyor belt. When I picked up my luggage, the official called to me, "Sir, come over here. We need to look in your suitcases."

I replied, "No, I'm on a tour group and need to catch my bus."

He insisted, "You come over here to be searched."

I repeated, "No, I'm in a hurry—I have to catch my bus!"

He came back with, "Come over here, NOW!"

The Lord intervened at that moment and a new Customs inspector appeared. I set my carry-on bag on the table and opened it. He spotted the books and asked, "What kind of books are these?"

I answered, "They're Bibles. I'm a Christian."

He said, "So am I."

I thought, *Is he really a Christian or is he just saying this?*

He asked a few questions like, "Where did these Bibles come from?"

I told him, "I speak in churches to raise money to buy these Bibles to bring to Cuba, plus other supplies to help the people of Cuba."

He asked if there were any more Bibles in the bags. I said, "No, not in this bag."

"Okay," he said, "Open up the next bag—the next suitcase."

I picked up the checked bag, weighing over 70 pounds, and opened it up. This one had 70 Bibles in it. When he saw all the Bibles, he started asking more questions, wanting to know where they had come from.

I told him again that I speak in churches to raise money. "I have come here to help the people of Cuba. Also, I have clothes and some medical supplies and child evangelism materials to teach the children about Jesus."

About then, the supervisor walked over. She was an older woman who looked mean and had a stern look on her face. She looked at me and saw the Bibles stacked up on the table. She said, "Confiscate all of the Bibles."

I objected saying, "Why do you hate Christianity so intensely? What is it about this Book that you hate so much?" I added, "Didn't even the Pope come to your country?"

She continued, "Take it all. Take all of his books. Take everything!" and she walked away.

I thought, *Lord, maybe I should have kept my mouth shut.* I prayed under my breath. *Lord, please touch her heart.*

The inspector, whose name was Pedro, said, "Please forgive me. I am married and have two children, and this is what I have to do."

I replied, "I am not offended. It is only right that you do your job. That's good! The Bible tells us to obey those in authority over us. Just as you're doing your job, I am also doing my job. My Heavenly Father has sent me to do the work of the Gospel, saying, 'Go into all the world and preach the Gospel to all people.' So you're doing your job and I am also doing my job."

He paused, "Wait a minute." He went back and talked to the woman who had just a few minutes ago told him to take all my stuff. He pleaded, telling her, "He raises money to buy Bibles; he has brought clothes for the kids and medical supplies to help us and materials to teach the children." I saw God change that woman's face right before my eyes. Suddenly, her stern, mean look softened, and a big smile appeared on her face.

She said, "Okay, let him go through with everything."

He came back and told me I could go. He said, "You can take all your stuff. She said it is okay."

I was so excited. No matter how many times you see the Lord work, it's always amazing! Only He is able to change someone's heart. Once again I saw Him move in a situation right before my eyes! All five of us men got through Customs that day. Also, there was a woman that we had given 50 Bibles to carry through Customs for us, so all together 550 Bibles made it through.

One of the guys on the team had contacts with a group of churches in Cuba. He asked the contacts to come to the hotel where we were staying and about 10 people came. The Latin culture is one that is not afraid to show affection. They were hugging and kissing us, so very glad to see us and to know that Christians from the United States had come to help them.

It was about 5 o'clock in the evening. The hotel was on the Malecon, the road which runs parallel to the ocean. I asked the contacts how they would like to move the Bibles.

Usually, we move Bibles in the dark of night, when no one is watching. They said, "Oh, just bring them down from the hotel room and we'll load them into our car."

In Cuba, they have large old cars from the 50's and 60's. We rode the elevator down to the lobby and walked outside with the Bible-laden suitcases. It was interesting— they were taking the Bibles out of the suitcases and loading them into the trunk of the car in broad daylight on one of the major streets in Havana!

When I saw this, I went up to the room and fell on my knees. I cried, "Oh, Lord, please help us! Please help us, Jesus; we're all about to go to jail today." I thought, *The Lord just got us through Customs and now all these Bibles are going to be confiscated by the police, and we will all be arrested.*

Meanwhile, the contacts said they could use all the medical supplies they could get, so we gave them two suitcases full. They were able to get all the Bibles and other materials safely to their church that night. They called to say how grateful they were for such a big load of Bibles and that they would be gone in a short time. They also told us that while they were loading the Bibles into the trunk of the car, two people came up and asked if they could each have a Bible.

I saw how the Lord had His hand on the situation and that I didn't need to worry. It was really amazing!

The men shared with us how in two months' time, 57 doctors and lawyers had come to Christ. They were really excited to get the medical supplies because even the best

Cuban hospitals can't get something as simple as aspirin. We talked to one pastor who had been to the dentist a couple of years before. He told us how there were three people in a row, sitting in dental chairs, and the dentist was passing instruments from mouth-to-mouth. Occasionally, he would wipe off the instrument with the same dirty cotton ball. The pastor said he didn't go to the dentist anymore—it just wasn't safe!

Taking Bibles and Gospel tracts through Customs isn't the only thing that can be difficult. On another trip, one of the church secretaries had asked us to bring a full Bible flannel graph set to help their house church.

Karl and I flew in with materials, and they caught me right away as they saw the Bibles in my carry-on. I tried to discreetly tell Karl that he would need to take most of the suitcases through Customs since I had already been caught.

When I walked up to the Customs desk, the young Customs officer told me to open my bag. I slowly opened the bag. It was obvious he had seen the Bibles and Gospel tracts. He asked me what they were and then told me to close up the bag. He went to talk to his supervisor. When he came back, he said," You need to give me some of the Bibles!" I gave him three and he asked for two more. Then he told me to close the bag.

He came back a few minutes later and said, "Give me some of the Gospel tracts!" I gave him some, and he asked for a few more, so I gave them to him. Then he told me to close my bag again.

In the meantime, Karl had been stopped in Customs with three bags. The woman told him to put the top suitcase on the table. She saw the flannel graphs and made him unpack them. Then she wanted to see the next suitcase, which also contained flannel graphs. She began to take them out.

When she wasn't looking, he would knock them onto the floor and then sneak them back into the suitcases. What Karl didn't know was that there was another Customs agent behind him, watching and laughing, but he never told the woman!

The last suitcase contained the full Bible flannel graph for the church secretary. The woman took it away from Karl. I was close by and pleaded with her to give it back. I told her that I had promised it to a friend. At one point, we both had our hands on it, and she said, "You cannot have it!" I said, "You can't have it!" Then she yanked it out of my hands.

I was so disappointed and frustrated. I left the Customs Hall and prayed, "God, please soften her heart. I ask for Your intervention." Twenty minutes later, Karl came out. He said, "I got your flannel graph back!" I was elated. When we gave the flannel graph to the secretary, I told her it was not only a spiritual battle to get it to her, but a physical battle as well.

The Lord's ways are certainly not our ways, but I'm learning to trust Him in all things. On another trip into Cuba, I was with a six-member team. Three of us made it through Customs with our loads. The other three had their Bibles confiscated. We were thankful for the Bibles that made it through and committed the other ones to the Lord.

When we were getting ready to leave the country, we decided to get the confiscated Bibles to bring to the Christians in Panama. At the Customs area, we asked if someone could help us get the Bibles. Everybody just looked at us and laughed—they weren't interested.

Then a younger man, in his late 20s, came over and said that he would help us. He was friendly, with a warm smile and very kind. He escorted us to collect the Bibles. Then, he followed us to the check-in counter to make sure we checked them in.

I asked him, "Excuse me, sir, could I give you a Bible?"

He said, "No, that's all right, I already have one. My mom is a Christian." I thought it was very interesting that they confiscated Bibles at their job and yet some had Bibles in their own homes.

I asked him, "Sir, if you were to die today, do you know where you'd spend eternity?" He wasn't certain. I shared the salvation message with him and then prayed with him. He seemed genuinely grateful.

We never know how God is going to use a frustrating situation, or even turn it around, especially when we go through Customs. Sometimes I need to count to ten under my breath, so I don't get angry or act in the flesh.

I can get frustrated by the injustice around the world, but I've learned to do what the Word tells us to do … be wise as a serpent, yet gentle as a dove … (Matt 10:16) and to be sensitive to the Holy Spirit's leading so that I say the right things. It may be an opportunity to share the Gospel and possibly lead someone to the Lord. Even though my flesh may want to get upset, I have to ask the Lord to help me respond the way He wants me to—with the love of Christ.

Cuba is a place full of people with a tremendous hunger for the Word of God. One church group we've been working with has more than 200 churches and they've seen over 10,000 people come to faith in Christ in just one year!

As you can see from these reports, this is a country that needs your prayers—so please join with me in praying for Cuba and its people!

# Chapter 14

# HUMAN TRAFFICKING

"The Spirit of the Lord God is upon Me, because the Lord has anointed Me to preach good tidings to the poor; He has sent Me to heal the brokenhearted, and proclaim liberty to the captives, and the opening of the prison to those who are bound; To proclaim the acceptable year of the Lord and the day of vengeance of our God, to comfort all who mourn" (Isaiah 61:1-2 NKJV).

These are the words Jesus chose to declare Himself to the world. This was His mission; this was His calling. As Christians, we are His disciples and we are called to continue in His footsteps.

There are 27 million modern-day slaves.[1] Illegally trafficked by means of force, fraud, coercion, and abduction—an unprecedented number are being sold into sex slavery all over the world. Each year, 12,000 victims are trafficked from Nepal into India's brothels alone.[2] Sex trafficking is increasing, and I believe God wants to use His Church to help change this problem.

Brothels litter many of the streets and alleys in the slums of Mumbai, Phnom Penh, Rio de Janeiro, and many others. These victims are forced to line the streets, advertising themselves. Most women are forced to serve up to twenty customers a day.

They live in deplorable conditions. Sickness is rampant throughout these brothels, and sadly, many become infected with AIDS. In a case study by Harvard School of Public Health, over 60% of young Nepalese sex slaves from Mumbai were infected with HIV.[3] These women and children are kept until they die, are killed, or in the case of a blessed few, are rescued.

Many years ago, while visiting contacts in Nepal, I had the privilege of meeting a few women who had been delivered out of sex slavery. They touched my heart and I immediately saw the need for God's Church to be actively involved in rescuing women and girls from sex trafficking.

I was humbled by their genuine love for their Savior Jesus Christ. They worshipped freely, hands raised and tears flowing down their cheeks—so grateful to be rescued from the darkness.

I believe God's people need to work on all fronts: educating villagers of the dangers of sexual predators and moving orphans off the streets into children's homes where they are loved, cared for, and raised as disciples for Jesus Christ. But we must also do everything we can to rescue the women and girls who have become trapped in the red-light districts. One woman said, "Please rescue us out of this hell-hole!" I believe Jesus would be in the darkest places, pulling them out of the pit and we should do the same.

Trapped in harsh cycles of poverty, and corrupted by cruel and hopeless religions, family members often sell their own wives, mothers, and children for as little as $10.00 U.S. dollars. I've met women who were sold by their own relatives into India's brothels.

Ladki was just one of these women. She was married in her Nepali village when she was only fourteen. When she discovered she had epilepsy, her husband divorced her. She went back to live with her family, who tried many treatments. Finally, her brother said he would take her to Mumbai for treatment.

"Truly, I trusted him," said Ladki. When they arrived in Mumbai, her brother sold her into a brothel. She discovered that her sister had also been sold in Bombay by her brother. Ladki's parents were aware of her brother's plans. "It was very bad and [the] worst place. Many customers used to come. I felt very bad and thought 'my life will be finished here.'"

Many girls from Ladki's village, both "big and small" were sold by their own brothers. "We used to sit and cry a lot. We had no hope." One day, our contact went to the brothel and shared the Word of God with them. The women believed, as did the brothel owner who set them free.

Ladki came home and shared the Gospel with her family. She has forgiven her brother and is restored with her parents, who have since become Christians. She is now serving the Lord.

Other women have told stories of good-looking young

men who came to their village and took an interest in them. The men said they loved them and wanted to marry them. After a time of courtship, they were married and the men took them to India for what they thought was their honeymoon; it was really to sell them as sex slaves.

In some areas, girls as young as five are kidnapped or even sold by their families. They enter the brothels at such young ages that they grow up not knowing anything, except a world of violence, deceit, and abuse. For many who are rescued, it takes years to understand that not all people in the world wish them harm. They learn to trust no one, to abandon emotions, and passively accept their torment. Nearly 2 million children are exploited in the global commercial sex trade every year.[4]

Only when the women are broken can they be trusted to stand in front of the brothels and lure the men in. They are broken by means of torture—being left alone in a locked "cage" or a room without windows, where they are starved, beaten, tortured and raped repeatedly until they are so full of fear that their spirit is broken.

The prettier a girl is, the more money she brings. I have heard stories of girls as young as five years old who are sold for a high price. Men with venereal disease or AIDS believe that if they have sex with these virgin girls they will be healed. They will pay up to $500.00 to use these little girls. After that, they are only worth about $10.00. Those who traffic these girls now have doctors "fix" them, so they can be resold at the higher price.

The women in the brothels are sold to the men for $10.00 for 10 minutes, while women over 50 bring about $5.00 for 10 minutes. These women are not prostitutes; they are sex slaves, sold against their wills, so others may profit from their bodies. I have met many of these women over the years and without Christ, they are hopeless. Their eyes are empty; they haunt you.

One contact we know ministered in the brothels in Mumbai and met a five-year-old girl who had been orphaned after her mother's death from AIDS. The little girl lived in a brothel where 10 women worked. She slept on a mattress under one of the bunk beds. A customer had used one of the ladies and then tried to grab the young girl and force himself on her. Fortunately, she was able to escape his grasp. After this, she was afraid to be around men.

Our contact asked the owner of the brothel if he could take the little girl to a safe place, as this was no place for her to grow up. The woman who ran the brothel refused to let her go, saying that she was all she had in this life. The girl's mother had given her daughter to the brothel owner before dying.

The brothel owner was in tears, knowing that this was no place to raise her; yet, she held on because this child was all she had in this world.

Our contact kept thinking of his own daughter, as the two girls were the same age. He grieved for several weeks. A few weeks later he received a letter from the woman saying that she had taken the girl to an orphanage two hours away from the city, where she would be safe and have a chance in life.

I heard another story about a Nepali girl who was orphaned when she was 8 years old after the death of her parents. She went to live with her aunt, who sent her to school for a few years with the intent of selling her later. Because the more educated girls can be sold to higher paying clientele, brothels will pay more to purchase them.

At the age of 12, she and her best friend were taken to Mumbai under the premise of a vacation and sold by the aunt for $600.00 each. The young lady was sold from brothel to brothel until she contracted Hepatitis. Often when these women and girls get sick, they just find an alley to lie down in and die.

Thankfully, she was taken to a hospital where a missionary family met her and ministered to her. She is now healed and serving the Lord.

The stories the victims tell are heart-breaking and move us to action. I am convinced that God's Church is to be involved in standing up for these women, girls, and boys. I have seen the police standing on the street corners in the red-light districts. They require money from the women; otherwise, they are thrown into prison to rot. I believe that God's people need to stand for those who cannot stand up for themselves.

Our ministry works with a wonderful sister in the Lord, who reaches out in a red-light district in Asia. She has set up a beauty parlor and ministers to the women who come into her shop. While they are in the chair, she is witnessing to them and praying for them. This woman is one of my heroes, as she faithfully ministers in a place that is hostile to the Gospel. She knows that is where God has placed her. She has received many death threats, but knows that Jesus is with her.

I am amazed at the difference God is making in this dark, oppressive, and repulsive area. Several years ago, when I first went there, you would look at the women and it was as if you could see right through them, almost like they were the walking dead. Now, as we walk down the street, the women's faces light up. They smile when they see our contact. They are anxious to greet her and ask for prayer. The darkness and hopelessness is fading from the faces of these women; they now smile and appear to have hope.

In one of the brothels, our contact had prayed for a woman who was very sick. She was healed by God's power and now all the women there, as well as the brothel owner, frequently ask for prayer. Even the physical appearance of the brothel has changed; it is now cleaner and lighter.

We have prayed for these things before, but now it's as if you can visibly see God changing hearts. He is lifting the oppression in this place. We have even heard reports that brothel owners are coming to faith in Jesus Christ, and they are forgiving the women and girls of their debts and closing the brothels down! Only God can do this!

One of the hardest things to see in the brothels is the children that are being raised there because their mothers are sex slaves. They are still innocent and have hope in their eyes, rather than the emptiness that marks the women. But we also know that if the girls do not get out of this area, they will become victims of sexual slavery.

Through our contact, the children are being ministered to and given hope. In the evenings, they come up to a classroom above the beauty parlor where they are offered free tutoring. In the bright classroom, with pictures of Jesus and Bible verses on the walls, they are shown love and taught the Truth of the Scriptures.

Her ministry team is having them memorize Scripture, teaching them to worship Jesus and pray, and also praying for them before they leave to return to the brothels. It has been on her heart to establish a night care outreach for these children as well. We are supporting this vision and working with her to provide a safe place for them to sleep during the darkest and most vulnerable hours in the red-light district.

I'm humbled every time I visit this ministry, as I see how God has radically changed a humble woman and entrusted her with a ministry that I believe is very near and dear to the heart of God. He is doing a mighty work to set captives free in the brothels of India!

Recently one of our Nepalese contacts visited a village. She exhorted the women not to sell their children into the brothels of India. Then the mothers began to cry, confessing that they had already sold their daughters because they needed the money. The police chief said that it needed to stop because there were no women left in the village for the young men to marry. Then I heard the report that sons were now selling their mothers and husbands selling their wives!

When we work to understand the root causes of the suffering of so many women and girls, we can begin to see opportunities for change. There are many factors that play into the acceptance of sex trafficking and forced prostitution. Religion plays a vital role in areas that are predominately Muslim, Hindu or Buddhist. This is mainly because women are often thought of as impure or inferior to men. This is why prostitution is sanctioned in the eyes of many.

Fierce poverty also plays a huge part in the increasing number of victims. With large families, parents are often forced to view children as commodities in order to provide for the rest of the family. In many areas, commercial sex has become more accepted, less shocking, and political corruption is rampant. An increase in industrialization has caused an economic growth, allowing a higher number of men to have the extra funds to buy sex.

Even while more and more laws are put into place, the number of women who are trafficked increases. We believe that if we can promote change in the cultural thinking, it will, in turn, cause a change in the statistics. It is important to educate the people of the risks involved in the sex trafficking industry and offer them hope in Jesus Christ.

We also think it is important to help provide options for families to create ways of income without having to resort to the unthinkable. It is imperative to get children off the streets and into safe homes before they are scooped up into this growing commercial sex industry.

It is estimated that 600,000-800,000 victims are trafficked internationally each year.[5] Women are forced to migrate to certain cities along the borders considered "high supply zones" as part of an organized trafficking network.

While India is bringing in Nepalese girls, they are sending thousands of women and children from India to the nations of the Middle East. Girls are often taken from their homes and illegally sold in another city as the customers want something "different or exotic." Many are promised good work in another country, but they arrive to discover they have been tricked into slavery. And now, they are there illegally, with no legal rights. They are far from home, with no one to stand up for them.

The women and girls rescued from trafficking bear deep emotional scars. They have learned to trust no one and to abandon their feelings. Those placed in aftercare centers often remain remote for years, and it is rare that a girl will quickly heal or connect with anyone.

The girls sent to secular aftercare centers progress slowly, if at all. It's our understanding that many end up back in the brothel system after leaving the centers. They do not know how to live as free people and often drift back to the only familiar thing they know. Many who come out of the system fall into prostitution simply because they know of no other way to support themselves. Even if they are rescued from their torment, but do not find salvation, they are no better off because their souls are in the same bondage as before.

In contrast, many of the women who go to Christian safe houses and come to know Christ find the peace that passes all understanding. The perfect love of God is the only thing that is strong enough to overcome such walls of bitterness and pain. As His presence heals each scar, the beauty of true joy radiates from His daughters. They find hope, forgiveness, and purpose.

The women are also taught a vocation, so they can support themselves. Some have returned to the brothel areas so that they can witness to others who remain trapped in sexual slavery.

Such is the testimony of Sarita and Babita. Sold by their own brother, these two sisters spent many years in Bombay's brothel system before being rescued. Now bold witnesses for Christ, they reach out to other women enslaved in the red-light district. Their faces are radiant for their Lord and Savior Jesus Christ! They opened a small tea shop and have done well in their own legitimate business. More recently, they became house mothers at one of our new safe houses. God is using them in tremendous ways to minister to women coming out of the red-light district!

We are working to reach more women and children trapped in sex slavery with the message of Jesus Christ and find long-term solutions to this epidemic problem. God has blessed us to open more safe houses, while we continue to support outreaches inside the red-light districts that rescue and minister to sex trafficking victims.

Whenever I see a movie about the Holocaust, I wonder what I would have done if I had lived in Nazi Germany. Would I have kept quiet while my neighbors were being taken away to the concentration camps? Would I have caved under pressure and joined with the Nazis, or would I have been like Corrie Ten Boom and her family who hid the Jews in their house? They paid a high price for saving the lives of those who were led to the slaughter.

In our day, we have a different opportunity to help those destined for destruction. Will we stand up for them? Or will we be complacent, and say, "Those poor women and girls, but it's not my problem?"

We are convinced that prayer is the key as we cry out to God and ask for His divine intervention. Will you join with us in prayer? Please ask God to change the hearts of all those who are involved in the sex trafficking business.

# Chapter 15

# DIVINE APPOINTMENTS

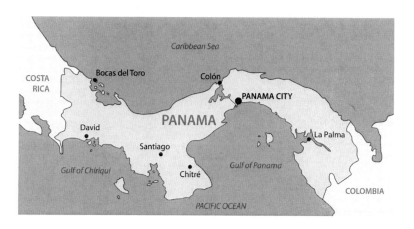

"To console those who mourn in Zion, to give them
beauty for ashes, the oil of joy for mourning, the garment
of praise for the spirit of heaviness; that they may be
called trees of righteousness, the planting of the Lord
that He may be glorified" (Isaiah 61:3 NKJV).

We flew down to Panama, in Central America, to minister
the Gospel and deliver Bibles. From there, we were flying to
Cuba to deliver Bibles to our contacts. There were six of us
on the team. One of the ladies who coordinated the team had
emigrated from Panama to America years before. Now, she
was showing us around, introducing us to some of the pastors

she knew.

We flew to Panama City and the next day we met a pastor who lived on the outskirts of the city. He and his wife were very gracious people. They really loved the Lord and were very zealous for Him. We had a great time getting to know them and ministering to their church.

We were invited to another church and a few people interested in receiving ministry from our team came to our hotel afterwards. One woman was from Colombia and she shared her story with us. She had come to Panama to get a job. At that time, Colombia was having a lot of problems with the drug cartel and unemployment was high. She was not a Christian.

When she arrived in Panama, she was forced into a life of prostitution; for 18 months she was made to work as a sex slave in a brothel. A little church down the street from that brothel was praying night and day for these girls to come to know Jesus. Her story of God's intervention was very interesting.

One day, God made a way of escape for her. The door, which was usually locked and always watched, was unattended. She had been trying for 18 months to get away from that brothel, and finally, she was able to do so … thanks to the Lord's rescue! She went to that little church and they were able to help her some, but she still needed more help. She decided to visit the church where our team met her for this reason. Her first time at the church was also the day of our visit, and she had come forward at the end of the service for us to pray for her.

She ended up staying with us in our hotel in Panama City and the team was able to minister to her on many levels. I learned the importance of perseverance in prayer when ministering to someone with deep issues. It takes time and I need to be patient. It was quite a battle—BUT JESUS—set her totally free from demonic activity. The Holy Spirit ministered to her and she just wept. She was very grateful for the work of God in her life.

Later, we were going to minister in the mountains that were north of Panama City. We invited this new convert to come along with us. Since we planned to be there for several days, we thought it would be a good opportunity to continue ministering to her.

The Lord really did a tremendous work in her heart and she helped minister to the people along with us. The Holy Spirit would touch others through her and they would just start to cry. She was also emotional, and cried at the idea that God would use her. We spent three days in the village and then returned to Panama City.

Since we were going to Cuba in two days, we thought about trying to help her get back to Colombia. She had a return airplane ticket, so we planned to take her to the airport to get her on a flight to Bogotá. The reason we thought it would be best to get her back to Colombia was because she had gone public with her story. She had incriminated some high level public officials, who had been her clients, by giving out their names.

She was on the front page of the newspaper for two days in a row. The article included her picture, along with her story. She even told how she had been forced into sex slavery. However, our timing was not the best—it was rush hour on a Friday night. It took us almost 45 minutes in a taxi to get across the city to the airport.

We took her to the airport and tried to get her on the flight. They approved to let her on that flight, but when we tried to send her through Immigration, the official recognized her name on the passport. He stated, "I can't let her go." He said, "I would like to let you go back to your country, but because you told your story to the newspaper, everybody is watching. If they found out that I let you through this border, I would lose my job."

It was a dead end, so I asked the Lord what we should do next. We took her back to the hotel and prayerfully tried to figure out another way. He guided us and again provided a way of escape for her! She was able to travel to Colombia by bus a few days later. Today, she is living with her mother and children.

On the way back to the hotel, we took another taxi. It was close to Mardi Gras time, or what they call "Carnival" in Central and South America. The driver was wearing a sombrero and had the radio on really loud; he was definitely ready to party. I got in the front seat next to him and the three women climbed into the back seat. The women and the driver spoke very good Spanish. My friend, Anna, asked me to have him turn the music down. He only turned it down a little, so I asked him to turn it off. I said, "We're Christians, and we really don't care for that kind of music."

My Spanish is not very good, but I felt really impressed to share the Gospel with this man. Anna translated as I witnessed to him. After we had been ministering to him for about ten minutes, he stopped for a red light and I saw him wipe a tear from his eye. He took off his sombrero, handed it to me and asked me to get rid of it. He didn't want it anymore. I thought, "Lord, what are you doing in this guy?" I shared with him a little while longer, but now it was becoming a pretty intense conversation.

Anna said, "Pat, why don't you stop for a while. We'll just take over from here, in Spanish." The woman who had escaped from the brothel started to talk to him in Spanish. She gave her testimony about how God had brought this group of six Americans down to Panama and they had ministered to her. She explained how she gave her life to Christ, and how God really set her free from demonic powers. She testified how God then worked through her to touch the people in the villages. She was crying as she was telling this story. She shared about how much God loved her to send a team from America to minister to her, to help deliver her out of bondage, and to bring the Gospel to her.

When we arrived at the hotel, I asked the driver if he was

ready to give his life to Christ. He said, "I am a backslidden Christian—I have been backslidden for two years. I want to give my life back to the Lord today. I have been miserable in sin and I am ready to give my life back to Jesus." We prayed with that man and he recommitted his life to Jesus. We had a great time ministering to him as he was very receptive and the Lord really touched him. He said, "I can't wait to get home to tell my wife and my kids that I got right with God today. They have been praying for me for two years."

We said, "We are going to Cuba tomorrow. Would you be able to give us a ride to the airport?" We thought we would help him by giving him some more business. We said, "We will probably need two taxis, because there are six of us, and we have lots of luggage."

He said, "Okay. I have a friend who also drives a taxi; I'll bring him."

At 6:00 in the morning, they were there to take us to the airport. We rejoiced for the opportunity to pray with this man, as we knew it was a divine appointment. Three of us rode in each taxi. We were in the taxi with our driver's friend, and the other group was ministering to our driver from the day before. I was sitting in the passenger seat, next to the driver. My friend, Elsa, and another friend were in the back seat. We all had our suitcases in the trunk.

We decided to stop at McDonald's, and we bought our drivers breakfast. Then we began the drive to the airport. I felt burdened to share the Gospel with this man. Elsa translated for me. As I started to share a little bit of the Gospel with him, I felt I should make it a little more personal.

I said, "Sir, what if your son came to you and said, 'Dad, I hate you, I love drugs, you are not my dad any more. I love drugs and I want to serve the devil?' How would you feel inside?"

The man was shocked and said, "How did you know? Last night, my wife and I were up all night long with our son. He came to us and said, 'Mom and Dad, I don't love you anymore. I'm addicted to drugs, and I want to serve the devil.' My wife and I have been up all night long, just crying and trying to figure out what to do. How did you know? How did you know?"

I said, "I don't know, but God knows." We were able to pray with that man to repent of his sins and put his faith and trust in Jesus.

He said, "How do I help my son?"

I said, "We're going to pray right now for your son. When you go home, pray together with your wife, pray for your son and that your whole family will serve Jesus. Tell your wife what you did today, that you gave your life to Jesus Christ, and your life is going to be based on His Word and obedience to Him."

He prayed for his salvation and then we prayed for his family. We knew that this was another divine appointment from the Lord. Both men lived in the same neighborhood as the first church we had ministered at, and they knew the pastor that was really on-fire for Christ. God was good to even provide them with a pastor, right there in their very own neighborhood!

# Chapter 16

# YOU'RE FREE TO GO

"You did not choose Me, but I chose you and appointed you that you should go and bear fruit, and that your fruit should remain, that whatever you ask the Father in My name He may give you" (John 15:16 NKJV).

On my first trip to Laos, I was traveling with two other men. Our plan was to initially bring in a small load of Bibles. We thought it would be wisdom to start small, until we could get a better understanding of the land and how things worked in the country. We traveled to northern Thailand and arrived at the Mekong River, where we loaded our luggage into a long canoe-type boat with a motor on it.

My heart was racing as we stepped off the boat. One just never knows what to expect when going through Customs. It's not only the laws that can create problems, but the temperaments of the individuals who work there. We walked up a hill to a small government building, where we had been told the Immigration and Customs Office was located.

The office was just a narrow room, with a desk and one official who stayed behind the counter. The space was only big enough for one person to enter at a time. We took turns stepping into the building as they stamped our passports. After all three of us had our passports stamped, they told us, "You're free to go." Those four words, "You're free to go," were like music to our ears.

There weren't any Customs security lines, only random checks if the man in the building deemed it necessary. After traveling to China, making many border crossings with Bibles and experiencing many harrowing situations, this was a relief.

While staying in the capital, Vientiane, we met some followers of Jesus who were in need of Bibles. This was the beginning of many years, by the grace of God, of delivering Bibles to the country of Laos—all in all—tens of thousands of Bibles. In all that time, only once did our team ever encounter a problem.

We were entering the country with a large load of tribal Bibles. We had placed sweaters on the top and sides of the bags, so they wouldn't look like they contained books. As we were walking through Customs, an agent decided he wanted to see inside one of the bags. He didn't seem that serious, so I told the team to just keep walking. We walked out of the airport, rented a van, and proceeded to load the bags into the van. I told the driver, "Go!"

He said, "The man in Customs wants to see the contents of the bags."

I was concerned. We couldn't go, but I didn't want him to look inside the bags either. I thought, Now, we're *stuck*. We decided to pray and trust the Lord.

We took a bag back into the airport. The official told us to open the top of the bag. When he looked inside, all he saw was the sweaters. He reached down into the bag about four inches, but all he could feel was the sweaters, so he cleared us to go. Had he reached a few inches more, he would have found the first Bible. God had prevailed once again.

There are many factors that contribute to the difficulty of bringing Bibles into a country. It's more than just getting past Customs. These bags can get very heavy when loaded down with Bibles. That weight, combined with the heat and humidity (especially in a country like Laos) can be difficult to transport. And yet, each time we get them through and deliver them, we are reminded of how worth it the work really is. The reaction and gratefulness of those who receive God's Word erases anything we might have gone through in the process.

One day, I was meeting our contact for lunch. I wanted to ask him if we needed to continue bringing him Bibles. Before I could even ask him, he said, "Please don't stop coming here. Other than you, there is only one other church from Australia that brings us Bibles! Many times, we have believers who walk for two weeks through the jungle to come and get these Bibles. If you had not come, we would have nothing to give them!"

He shared how several times, right after our teams had dropped off Bibles, the believers would show up. Sometimes it would be the very next day. He said he would break down and weep, thanking God for His provision.

I also got my answer. Yes, we need to keep carrying Bibles in!

On another trip, we brought in 166 Lao Bibles. These are very big Bibles, weighing about three pounds each. I had two women with me and the three of us carried this large load of Bibles into the country. We went to our contact's office, where I remember having to carry them upstairs in the high heat and humidity. The next morning I needed to write an e-mail, so I went to our contact's office to use his computer at 8:00.

While I was there, he said that I needed to meet some tribal Christians who were visiting his office. He shared how these women take great risk to deliver God's Word to the remote villages. I was so humbled to meet these servants of the Lord. Their faces were radiant, as love for Jesus was evident on their countenances. They could be imprisoned or killed for their work, but they believe helping the persecuted Church is more important than their personal safety.

I returned to the computer work, and 30 minutes later, he had another person for me to meet. This man was an evangelist, who was returning from an area where many tribal villages had repented and wanted to serve Jesus. This man also took great risks to evangelize these remote villages. He was full of God's love and joy, too! He asked if our friend had any Lao Bibles, and our contact retrieved one from his office.

When the evangelist saw the Bible his eyes opened wide. It was the first time he had ever seen a complete Bible before. He shared how excited he was because he wanted to teach from the Old Testament in the villages, but couldn't before now. He asked if our friend had any more. Our contact took him into the office and showed him the other 165 Bibles. You would have thought it was Christmas as I watched his face light up—just knowing there were many more Bibles to help the hungry Christians!

As an added blessing for our team, one Sunday we attended a church meeting and saw some Christians using the Bibles we had carried in. It brings great joy to my heart to see followers of Jesus reading and studying God's Word! I am always encouraged by the gratefulness of the believers who receive the Bibles we bring them, but I'm also greatly encouraged at God's faithfulness to open borders and make a way for our teams. It is so evident that He wants His Word in these countries even more than we do.

I have seen the faithfulness of God time after time. For example, on one trip, we brought in 18 suitcases that were full of materials, and that didn't include our personal belongings. That was a lot of luggage! When the Customs officer came out of his office and saw all the bags, a puzzled look came on his face. I prayed, "Lord Jesus, please help us!" Just then, he turned right around and went back into his office. Then he started talking with another man. I told the team, "It's time to move!" We walked right past the guard, who was totally oblivious to what we were doing.

We delivered this large load of Scriptures and songbooks to a pastor, who had arrived at our guesthouse under the cover of darkness. When we opened the bags and showed him the materials inside, he did everything he could to keep from crying. He said, "Thank you for loving our people; thank you for caring about us!"

We asked him how else we could help. He said they needed more Bibles. He shared that they had 2,500 new believers, but they needed God's Word for them.

A few weeks later, a team of five men and I traveled to Laos carrying 400 Bibles—weighing 1,200 pounds. We were able to walk right through Customs and give them to our friends. They were very grateful.

My team was so motivated that we decided to go back to Thailand and get more Bibles. We had 500 more shipped to the border and then we went to Thailand to load them into bags. Normally, when we are crossing from Thailand into Laos, we have to transfer our bags from vehicle to vehicle, and then carry them across the Customs area. Truthfully, it's not easy lifting 1,500 pounds, regardless of whether they are Bibles or something else. As we were unloading them from the truck, a man in a van pulled up and said, "Do you need a ride to the capital?"

I inquired, "How much?"

He said, "$30," and I agreed.

As we were loading the bags filled with Bibles into the back of his van, he asked, "Are these Bibles, and are you Christians?"

I said, "Say what?" and acted like I didn't understand his question.

He said, "Don't worry, my wife is a Christian!" and this Buddhist man drove us across the border.

He could have easily turned us into the police, but he didn't and we were grateful! When we pulled up to the Customs inspection area, I thought for sure we would get caught. The back of the van was sagging very low. The cargo load of the van was filled from floor to ceiling with 500 Bibles. The Customs agent asked that we open the trunk of the van. I prayed in desperation, "Lord, we need your help!" The Customs agent looked in the van, and said, "Close it up, you're good to go!" God's mercy never fails! I can't wait to see in Heaven what that man saw in the van!

Since that time, our teams have been committed to

carrying even larger loads of Books in to help our brothers and sisters. The Lord honors the faith commitment to bring the Bibles in, and He opens the way before us.

Many years ago, our contact asked if we would help provide sweaters for 400 little orphan boys in the mountains. The temperature would drop to 40 degrees at night and all they had to wear were shorts and t-shirts. We gathered the sweaters and jackets and transported them to those in need.

In the process, we mentioned that we had a seed project that would help provide seed packets for the Christians work, so they could become self-supporting. They were very interested and another form of ministry was opened for us.

We gave them various types of seeds, including beets. When they planted the beet seeds, they had no idea what beets were. When the beets matured, they were afraid of them. They pulled them out of the ground and threw them off to the side for the animals. When our contacts visited them in the village, they saw the beets in a pile and asked what was happening. They said they didn't know what they were and were scared of them, so they were feeding them to the animals. The contacts taught them how to cook the beets and now they love them.

We also brought watermelon and cantaloupe seeds. Since they had never seen these fruits before, the contacts had to teach them how to eat them. And now they love cantaloupe and watermelon, along with the beets.

Opium production has dropped because they can grow vegetables instead, and the kids are growing larger than their parents. God is blessing the seed project, so we can help feed people around the world. It is amazing how God can use a simple thing like vegetable seeds when it's offered for His glory, to expand His Kingdom and further His purposes! We are not only bearing the life-changing spiritual fruit that remains, but natural fruit as well.

# Chapter 17

# EXPERIENCE DOESN'T ALWAYS MAKE IT EASIER

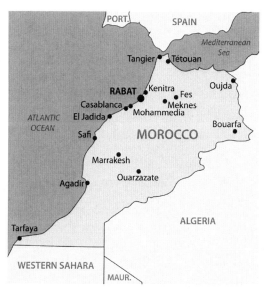

"This righteousness from God comes through faith in Jesus Christ to all who believe. There is no difference, for all have sinned and fall short of the glory of God, and are justified freely by his grace through the redemption that came by Christ Jesus" (Romans 3:20-24).

My friend warned me that Customs in Morocco was very difficult to get through. Ron had been there before, but this was my first trip and I was nervous. Though I appeared calm on the outside, I was trembling inside.

I can say that it has gotten easier over the years. The Lord has taken away many of my fears, but my stomach still gets a little nervous when I carry Bibles into closed nations. The closer I get to the country, the more nervous I feel. I think the anticipation is the most difficult part, not knowing what will happen. This is when you really have to trust God to make the way because ordinarily there simply wouldn't be one.

We took a four hour ferry ride from Spain across the Strait of Gibraltar. Porpoises swam alongside the vessel and we enjoyed the beautiful scenery of Spain's southern coast along the way, including the famed Rock of Gibraltar. As we approached Northern Africa, we noticed a marked difference. The houses and businesses of Tangier looked helter-skelter compared to the beautiful homes of southern Spain.

Ron and I separated on the ferry so if one of us was caught, the other could still get through. I was ahead of him and started a conversation with two other English-speaking men. We were talking casually as we walked through a building past two Moroccan men in uniform. They were not interested in us at all, so we kept talking and walking until the next thing I knew, we were outside the building. It was then that I realized we had just walked straight through Customs! I was so relieved and grateful to the Lord for opening the way!

We walked to the train station with our load of precious cargo and boarded a train headed south to reach some of the larger cities. The train filled up quickly as the departure time approached. A young Moroccan man asked if he could sit in the compartment with us, so we gladly invited him in. As we traveled, this young man started asking questions. Before long, he turned the conversation to religion and asked if we were Christians. We told him that we were, but all the while knowing he could be a plant who was trying to find out what we were doing in Morocco.

He shared some of his Islamic beliefs, which denies Jesus as the Son of God, along with His crucifixion and resurrection. He said he believed Jesus was a prophet. I questioned why he thought that was true. He replied, "Because the prophet Mohammad said he was."

I asked if he had ever read the New Testament; he said he hadn't. Then I said, "What if I told you that my friend Ron here is a prophet? You've never met Ron. You've never heard anything Ron has said, or read anything he has written. How would you know if I was telling you the truth? Maybe I'm deceived, or maybe I misunderstood Ron's message. Maybe *Jesus* … is more than a prophet."

The Lord touched his heart, and he said, "I understand; I need to read Jesus' writings for myself and not take the Prophet Mohammad's word for it." He said he would find Jesus' book and read it. We could not give him a Bible right then because it would have jeopardized the rest of the Bibles we had.

On my next trip to Morocco, I again traveled by ferry to

Tangier. I was expecting to see the same Customs building I went through the first time, but our vessel pulled into a different dock. To my surprise, it was a completely new set-up. We were told to walk through a huge parking lot area, which had to be about two miles long. Was I ever grateful for a roller bag with wheels, as my suitcases were heavily loaded with the "JESUS" videos!

While we walked through the parking lot, a security guard directed us to a small building I hadn't seen before. The officials called us over and ordered us to put our bags on the table in front of them. My heart was pounding, and I was thinking, *Today is the day I get arrested in Morocco!* As I was lifting my suitcases onto the table, the man in charge said, "Ah, forget it. Have a nice day."

Immediately, I thanked the Lord under my breath and quickly turned and walked out the door. In some ways, I was still afraid he might change his mind.

Later, I traveled to Morocco with a board member who has a heart for evangelism. Karl is always a joy to travel with. We loaded our bags with Gospel tracts, the "JESUS" film in Arabic and other native languages, and cassette tapes in the local dialects. We made it safely through Customs, and after settling down in the city, we set out to distribute the materials. Karl and I were both surprised by the people's receptiveness to the Gospel.

We distributed many materials on the streets and people would actually ask for more to share with their family and friends. After seeing what we were giving out, a group of young men approached us; all of them were interested and wanted literature. I finally opened my backpack and gave them everything I had. They literally cleaned us out. We were very encouraged to see this response to the Gospel! We traveled through other cities, giving out materials, and found that people were just as equally receptive to the Gospel.

One day, we decided to travel to some Berber villages. We had several cassette tapes and two "JESUS" films left in Tachelhit, the local Berber language. While checking into a guesthouse, a young Berber man approached us. He asked if we wanted a walking tour of the local villages the next day. Normally, this wasn't something we did, but we felt like it might be an opportunity from the Lord. In our prayers, we always ask God for divine appointments.

The next morning after breakfast, we started out on our walking tour. Karl liked to listen to praise music, so he had his Walkman on while we walked. The young Muslim man inquired what Karl was listening to. He had no idea what worship was, so I suggested that Karl let him hear. He put the headset on and started listening, but it didn't make sense to him. I suggested letting him listen to one of the Gospel cassettes in his language.

He started to listen to the Gospel presentation and was surprised it was in his dialect. We were walking along, and after listening for a few minutes, he commented, "This is good." A little later, he said, "This is really good." Then, a short time later, he said, "This is excellent, I really like this!"

After walking for about 45 minutes, we came to the first village. There were four young Muslim men sitting under a tree. They knew our guide, and asked, "What are you listening to?" He replied, "Listen to this, it's in our language!" The men listened to the cassette for a few minutes and then asked if they could each have a copy. We gave them all cassettes. They thanked us, and we moved on.

About 30 minutes later, we approached another village. Like the former village, there were three young Muslim men sitting under a tree talking, but the leader of the mosque was also there. He asked our tour guide what he was listening to, so the guide let him listen for a few minutes. He said he wasn't interested and walked away. The other three men asked if they could listen. Their response was different; they requested copies of the cassette tapes. We gave each man a cassette and then moved on.

By the time we approached the third village, our guide had already listened to the cassette two times. He was really impressed! Once again, there were young Muslim men that our guide knew and they were curious about what he was listening to. He was open to share it with them as well, and they also asked for the cassettes! We gave out the last one we had, and they thanked us. Then we headed back to the village where we were staying.

On the way back, the tour guide was so excited. He asked, "Do you have anything else in my language, so that I can learn more about this Jesus?" I pulled out the "JESUS" film in his dialect from my backpack. He was so excited! He asked if he could have two, and explained, "My in-laws have a VCR. They live up in the mountains, about four hours away. I would like to have one for me, to go up there and watch it, but I would also like to be able to give them one when I'm done." It was the last of the materials that we had. We thanked the Lord, that through this young man, we were able to get the Gospel into more villages!

# Chapter 18

# ARRESTED IN MOROCCO

What then shall we say to these things? If God is for us, who can be against us? He who did not spare His own Son, but delivered Him up for us all, how shall He not with Him also freely give us all things? Who shall bring a charge against God's elect? It is God who justifies. Who is he who condemns? It is Christ who died, and furthermore is also risen, who is even at the right hand of God, who also makes intercession for us. Who shall separate us from the love of Christ? Shall tribulation, or distress, or persecution, or famine, or nakedness, or peril, or sword? As it is written: 'For Your sake we are killed all day long; We are accounted as sheep for the slaughter.' Yet in all these things we are more than conquerors through Him who loved us. For I am persuaded that neither death nor life, nor angels nor principalities nor powers, nor things present nor things to come, nor height nor depth, nor any other created thing, shall be able to separate us from the love of God which is in Christ Jesus our Lord"
(Romans 8:31-39 NKJV).

After spending a week in Romania, our team of four traveled to Casablanca. We met up with seven other people who had carried in a large number of Arabic New Testaments, Gospel literature, and the "JESUS" film on VHS and DVD. By the grace of God, the whole team made it successfully through Customs!

A day later, our team headed south by train to a large city and prayer-walked the souk area, a hotbed for occult activity. It's a large open-air marketplace with vendors, fortune tellers, and snake charmers—sometimes referred to as a "carnival" for the occult. We were told many Christians were killed for their faith in this city during the 11th Century. We asked the Lord to forgive the city for its bloody history, especially against God's people.

Morocco has more than 30 million people, but there were less than 500 converts from Islam when we visited. As discouraging as that was, we found people very receptive and had many opportunities to share Christ with people.

We walked around the large square, asking God for His presence to be manifested through His Holy Spirit on the Muslims there and for many to come to faith in Jesus Christ.

Afterwards, we started to give out Arabic New Testaments. Many were interested, especially the young people. They thanked us and some even hugged us.

However, not everyone was receptive to the Gospel. One young man took a New Testament and deliberately tore it apart, right in front of us. He angrily threw the shreds of paper into the wind. It was heart-breaking and difficult to see this young man with empty eyes shredding God's Word.

The team decided to break into smaller groups and continue passing out literature. The Islamic call to prayer had just sounded, and people were going into the mosques. I was amazed at how receptive they were, even during this time. People would ask, "Can I have two more for my family?" or "Can I have two more for my friends?"

Still, there was opposition. As I gave a beggar some money with one of the New Testaments, a man came over and remarked, "What are you giving that garbage away for? Get out of here!" and he flung the New Testament right at a girl's face from my group. Fortunately, it missed her, but he was very hostile.

When we walked away, a mother with two small children followed us for about a block. Finally, she approached us and asked, "Sir, can I please have one of those books? Can I have one, please?"

We had just given away our last one, so I told her, "We don't have any more; I am really sorry."

She said, "Oh, I really wanted that book so bad!" It was disappointing to leave her empty-handed. Throughout our time in Morocco, we saw people like her—earnestly seeking Truth and desiring God's Word.

As one of our groups prayed about who they should give their last Bible to, they saw a woman and felt led to offer it to her. While doing so, they caught the interest of some people passing by. This drew a crowd, and they spontaneously began sharing the Gospel in Arabic. As a crowd quickly gathered, it also caught the attention of the police, who came and took them to the police station.

While they were being held, they testified and shared the Word of God. After 45 minutes, the police chief told them, "You are giving me a headache … just go." As they left, one young man on the team noticed they were being followed by the secret police. He split up from the others and wandered around, trying to lose them. After he was sure he was no longer being followed, he returned to the hotel. The team spent time praying through the situation, and the group rejoiced that God had given them the opportunity to share the Gospel and experience persecution for the name of Christ!

The next day our team visited some mountain villages, where people were very receptive as we shared the Gospel materials with them. Suddenly, the police arrived and watched us for a while, trying to convince us they were there for our protection. They escorted us back to the city and then left us.

We decided to have dinner downtown, which was an area of the city we had never been to before. We brought some literature to give out, but tried to be more subtle about it. Only two of us carried materials in our backpacks. Once again, the young people were very responsive to the Gospel and asked for additional books to share with those who were close to them.

After distributing the New Testaments, we began our walk back to the hotel. Suddenly, we were surrounded at a street corner by secret police in street clothes. They were very abusive toward the team, yelling at us, and demanding to see identification. They immediately began to push and shove the young man who had been questioned the night before.

I wasn't sure they were really police, so I asked to see their ID's. They showed us a card of some kind, but it was in Arabic, which I couldn't read. Then they showed us their guns, trying to intimidate us. The chief officer was very rude and aggressive. They arrested the two men from our team who they caught giving out literature. Afterwards, he insulted us by mouthing some very nasty words.

The two team members were held overnight at the police station. However, God still worked through their circumstances, and they were able to share the Gospel with all the police officers. They even led one of them to the Lord in the middle of the night! God also used a situation involving the young man to soften the chief officer's heart. In the end, he responded graciously to us.

Throughout this time, we were in constant communication with the U.S. Embassy. The next morning, our team was escorted to the airport by two undercover policemen. The two men arrested were deported through Immigration, while the remainder of our team had to make the necessary ticket adjustments to fly out sooner. Over the next 36 hours, we were all able to get on flights out of the country. Everyone arrived safely back in the United States.

While this was a frightening experience for all of us, the Lord's presence was always with us and His grace was extremely evident. We thank the Lord for the opportunity to experience a small part of the persecution that our brothers and sisters experience around the world. We would ask for you to please pray for those in Islamic countries who are still persecuted for the sake of the Gospel!

# Chapter 19

# SEWER KIDS RECEIVE CHRIST

"Pure and undefiled religion before God and the Father
is this: to visit orphans and widows in their trouble and
to keep oneself unspotted from the world"
(James 1:27 NKJV).

I was really excited when God gave me the opportunity
to make a trip to Romania. On my first trip, I took along a
team of five people with twenty duffel bags full of supplies.
I had heard how oppressive the government was under
Ceausescu, and that there were many orphans and widows.

Plain and simple, people were struggling just to survive.

We had purchased leftover seeds from a seed company, and in the load there were some flower seeds. When we got the seeds, I thought, "Lord, why did we get flower seeds? We don't use them." But before going to Romania, I had an opportunity to visit with a man who had been there previously. He shared with me that they really needed clothes and vegetable seeds, but if I had any flower seeds, to bring them as well. He said that during the Communist leader's reign, the people were not allowed to grow flowers because they represented hope. I immediately knew why God had given us the flower seeds.

We arrived late at night and successfully made it through Customs with 20 duffel bags full of supplies. We had to hire four taxis to carry all of the supplies and people to our hotel. The next morning, we had breakfast, and I called our first contact. She had a site on the Internet that said she was rescuing kids off the streets, and had been recommended by a man I knew.

However, once we met this woman, we all felt like something was wrong. We talked with one of her staff members, and were filled in on the truth; the ministry was a sham. It's a frustrating situation when anyone will cheat another, but it's especially grievous when people use widows and orphans.

Our other contact was from Christ For The Nations, so we were excited to connect with them. We were blessed to see how God was using them in Brasov, and we were able to distribute the supplies to many in need through their ministry.

The people had been oppressed by Communism for many years. We ministered to some widows that only made $20.00 a month. They said that after they paid their rent and heating bill, there was no money left for food, clothing, or anything else. The man we worked with had a team who would bring the widows to church once a month, feed them a really nice meal, and give them special attention. Then, before they left, the church would give them food and toiletries.

We were blessed to get a turn at giving the widows special attention. One woman from our team cut and styled their hair for them, while another woman polished their nails. They had never received such kind treatment before and many of the ladies cried.

We also went to the orphanages to spend time with the kids and play with them. It was a sad experience. At one point, I saw a little boy under a table. I walked up to the table and stretched out my hand to him. He went ballistic, screaming; he had never been touched before.

Even though it was painful to see children like this, it's good to go and be an ambassador for Jesus, and have the opportunity to share His love. There are many opportunities to minister if we will be open to the Holy Spirit's leading.

On one of our trips, we ministered to a unique group of Romas, which are known as gypsies. The people were very poor and had come to the northern part of Romania to work. Their jobs were to make bricks out of clay. Our team quickly blended with the people as we ministered to them.

We were invited back on a Saturday night to share the Gospel around a bonfire. Several young people from the church came and led worship with their guitars. We sang and had a good time with them. Then, I was asked to share my testimony and the Gospel message. Thankfully, I had an interpreter.

Afterwards, there were two men who wanted to repent of their sins and put their faith in Jesus Christ. We prayed with them for salvation. A married couple also prayed to recommit their lives to Jesus. The next day, they brought nine children to the church in Lipova to be dedicated to the Lord.

When we had finished praying for those who responded to the message, they asked us to pray over the river. The water level was very high and their village was in danger of being flooded.

On Monday morning, we went to the market. We had been asked by one of the elders to purchase some supplies that this village needed. We bought soap, shampoo, cooking oil, and other supplies. The pastor said they would give them fruit and vegetables from the greenhouses at the orphanage as well. We loaded all these supplies, which were quite numerous, in the back of the truck and drove out to the Roma village.

One of the two men who received salvation on Saturday night was standing by the roadside when we pulled up. His face lit up when he saw us. One of the team members got out of the truck and handed him a bar of soap. When she put the soap in his hand, the man's eyes immediately filled with tears;

then he broke down and started to cry.

When he gained his composure, he said, "On Saturday night, I repented of my sins and chose to trust Jesus as my Lord and Savior. Yesterday morning, I was taking a bath before going to church and I ran out of soap. So I prayed my first prayer to God, 'Lord, I need some soap.' Then you came to the village and gave me a bar of soap. God heard my prayers."

He was later given a Bible in the Romanian language, and when he received God's Word, tears welled up in his eyes again; he hugged and kissed the Bible!

The people in the village led us over to see the river. God had intervened and the river had dropped about three feet in less than 36 hours. They were praising God for His answer to prayer!

One thing that really tugged at my heart was seeing the street kids, especially those who live in sewers and are addicted to drugs. In Romania, there are lots of street kids, and many of them have to sleep in the sewers in the winter in order to stay warm. I wanted to see this for myself. One night, in the middle of December, I went out to the streets of Brasov with two other people. One was a Roma named Robert, whose wife had made up a gallon jug of hot tea and a big bag of sandwiches for our night ministry trip.

It was about 6:00 p.m. There was about nine inches of snow on the ground and it was really cold. We headed down to the railway station to minister to the street kids, but when we looked around, we didn't see any. Honestly, I was disappointed. I thought we had missed out on a ministry opportunity.

Robert said, "Come with me," and we walked about 100 yards to an open sewer. He called down into the sewer. About a minute later, three boys came climbing up out of it. They immediately hugged Robert, exclaiming how glad they were to see him. We gave them sandwiches and hot tea; then they bowed their heads and gave thanks to God for the food before eating. I couldn't help but think about how so many kids in America are blessed to live in nice homes, have good food and clothes to wear, but never once bow their heads to give thanks. These kids were truly grateful!

We then walked about one mile, along the railroad tracks, until we came to another open sewer. Robert called down into this sewer and nine kids came climbing out of it. They were wearing big baggy clothes, which were very dirty. There were eight boys and one girl. They said that their sewer was better because they had a mattress and a radio in it. Once again, they hugged Robert right away, and thanked both the Lord and us. They were so grateful that we cared enough to visit them and bring food to them. It's always a joy to minister to people who are grateful for help!

Years ago, I had a team of eight who were planning to go with me to Romania. A woman in the church, who wasn't a part of the team, said to one of the team members, "I don't know how you can go over there and spend two weeks with those kids and not get emotionally attached to them. How can you leave them? That would just rip my heart out." That mindset started with one woman, but it eventually spread to the whole team. The next thing I knew, nobody wanted to go on the trip!

We all have been given a choice of whether to stay in our comfort zones. For me, the choice is to be like Peter. I want to get out of the boat and see God work. It's easier to do nothing, or to criticize and make excuses—than it is to decide, "I'm going! I want to be an ambassador for Jesus and to trust God." He is always faithful when we make the step. He wants to use us as vessels of His compassion to those in need.

I really like going to the orphanages and spending quality time with the kids. Sometimes, we go to the old folk's home and minister to the elderly. On one trip, we took supplies to them and led twelve people to Christ while we were there. Our team was blessed. The administrator of the home would grab me by the arm, and say, "Come! Talk to this person! Talk to this person!" She took us all over the place. We just had a great time as we shared Christ and prayed with people; they were so receptive.

Then we went next door to a huge Catholic Church, where people were coming to pray for healing in their bodies. We met a woman and her son. I asked the elder from the church if he would translate and he said yes. We shared the Gospel with this woman and her son, and they both got saved. She said, "I came here to pray to the saints to get healed, and I met Jesus instead! I don't need to stay here!"

In Lipova, our contact pastors a church and oversees the orphanage we visit. We have been working with Pastor Moses for many years now. When we first visited the orphanage, they had a big greenhouse that was sitting empty. I inquired why they didn't grow vegetables and he said they couldn't get good seeds. The next trip we made to Lipova, we gave the orphanage seeds. When we returned, they had seven-foot-high tomato plants loaded with tomatoes and a huge vegetable garden outside. They said that they had fed the kids for the whole year, canned vegetables, helped the elderly, and sold $1,600 dollars worth of produce.

They told us that the greenhouses were the best thing they had ever done. I asked them what they wanted to do next. They said they wanted to build a second greenhouse and heat them both, so they could grow vegetables all year long. I asked how much it would cost. They said, "$18,000-$20,000 dollars." We prayed with them for God to supply their needs. Six weeks later, we received an e-mail telling us that they had found a used greenhouse; it was only $4,000 dollars. We told them to go ahead and buy it and sent them the money for it. When we returned, it was full of six-foot-high eggplants, loaded with vegetables!

In Romania, we can openly minister to people and God touches our team members when they go there. I think the simplicity of the life in Lipova, combined with the hard work, good fellowship and freedom to worship, seems to really change people. We are committed to helping them long-term, until they can get on their feet and help others. We are increasing our outreach to the Romas, as it shows people that we really do care about them.

Each country we minister in is different, and we must pray and ask God's direction for the strategies for each country. We have found that as we go with a servant's heart, God grants us favor and opens doors that no man can close. We are able to help strengthen the Church, encourage the believers, and reach out to the lost.

# Chapter 20

# IT IS FINISHED

"Are they servants of Christ?—I speak as if insane—I more so; in far more labors, in far more imprisonments, beaten times without number, often in danger of death. Five times I received from the Jews thirty-nine lashes. Three times I was beaten with rods, once I was stoned; three times I was shipwrecked, a night and a day I have spent in the deep. I have been on frequent journeys, in dangers from rivers, dangers from robbers, dangers from my countrymen, dangers from the Gentiles, dangers in the city, dangers in the wilderness, dangers on the sea,

dangers among false brethren…If I have to boast, I will boast of what pertains to my weakness"
(2 Corinthians 11:23-26, 30 NASB).

At one point, I thought I was supposed to move to Pakistan to work with a Bible college. It was my first time to make a trip alone to this country, but I was given the names of some people I could work with. There were many difficulties along the way, but the biggest disappointment was finding out that the Bible School, which claimed to have 2,500 students, was a total sham. Money was being raised in the States to support a work that didn't even exist.

In the meantime, I had been staying with some people who claimed to follow Jesus, but I think their whole motive was greed. The leaders of the group were very corrupt and became very controlling. They wanted to tell me what to do in every situation, seeing me as an opportunity to get to the American Church for money. This situation was very disturbing. By the grace of God, I was able to escape their control. I stayed with a missionary in an undisclosed location for my last two days in Karachi.

The leader of their group knew when I was leaving Pakistan to fly back to Hong Kong. The morning I flew out, during my prayer time I kept having the word "drugs" come to mind. I wasn't sure if that meant they might try to plant drugs in one of my bags or what, but I felt that it was a clear warning from the Lord. I asked my missionary friend if he would take me to the airport and make sure I had made it safely inside before driving off. Thankfully, I did make it safely out of the country and I have never seen those men again.

Years later, I heard the leader of a big ministry threatened to plant drugs in another believer's house in order to destroy his ministry.

I have made several trips to Pakistan throughout the years, but one trip really stands out to me. I was traveling with two friends and our plans for the day were to visit this village. The leader of the team had not told me previously about the situation we would face. We pulled up to the owner's house, which was very sparse, and there was a mud wall around the property.

We were led into the house, and as typical of Pakistani hospitality, were served milk tea. We met the owner of the home and his family. Then we were introduced to a lady and her four children. The woman seemed very shook up and was crying a lot, her eyes were red and puffy. The three younger children appeared completely oblivious to what was happening.

As time went on, I was able to piece together the situation. The lady's husband was a pastor named George, who had been directed by God to plant a church in a Muslim village. He obeyed the Lord and moved his family to the village.

The places of worship in Muslim countries have loud speakers, which they use to call people to prayer five times a day. This pastor decided he would put a loud speaker on top of his house, so others in the village could hear the Gospel when Christians came to worship.

This was a very courageous decision. Life is difficult for Christians in Pakistan, who often endure physical attacks, false accusations, and grave social mistreatment. Churches are routinely burned or destroyed. Christian ladies are forced to marry Muslim men, or they're attacked and disfigured. In the court system, Christians have no rights, and under Sharia Law (Islamic Law) the oppression is even greater. They are complete outcasts in their culture.

Pastor George was successful in his outreach to the Muslims, who would come to him for prayer. Many times, after ministering in Muslim areas, God would answer his prayers and the Muslims would return to ask more questions about Jesus. The village chief hated Pastor George and threatened to kill him, but Pastor George was not deterred because he wanted to be obedient to the call God had put on His life.

Pastor George continued to preach the Gospel and minister to those around him. One night, he and his wife and their four kids all huddled on the bed to watch the "JESUS" film in Urdu, their native language. By the time they finished watching the movie, the three younger ones had fallen asleep. George's wife got up from the bed and opened the door. There were two gunmen standing there. They came into the one room house, put a gun to George's throat, and shot him in front of his family. He fell back on the bed and said, "It is finished." He died right there in the presence of his family.

We were now in a different village, where his wife's in-laws lived, meeting his family just two weeks after this had happened. I could feel their grief and pain as I sat in the room with them. The mother was distraught, wondering how she would provide and care for the children. The two men I traveled with made sure that she and her children would be provided for financially. She was safe in this Christian village and could stay there with her relatives.

But what touched me the most was seeing the oldest son in the corner of the room. He was ten years old. When we first met him, he was huddled with his mother and younger siblings. Now he had gravitated off to the side, surveying the situation, fully realizing that he was now the 'man' of the family. I think he was watching us to make sure that his mother and siblings were not in danger, but at the same time wondering why these foreign men were there. I think he was also suffering in silence, having seen his dad martyred for the cause of Christ just two weeks before.

My heart went out to him, so I walked over and put my arm around him. I pulled him close to me; he didn't resist. I asked him his name and he told me. I then asked if we could pray for him and he agreed. We all three laid hands on him and prayed for him. Then I asked, "What do you want to do when you grow up?" He immediately answered, "I want to be a pastor like my Daddy!" Those words hit me like a ton of bricks!

He had seen his dad move their family to a Muslim village

in obedience to God's call. He had seen his dad faithfully preach, in spite of opposition from the village chief. He had just witnessed his daddy giving his life for the Gospel—and he wanted to follow in his dad's footsteps! I thought, *How do you stop people like this?* They live only to please Jesus and bring Him glory!

This is how the Church grows in Muslim countries. Christians are so devoted to following Jesus, even if it is at great risk to their own lives. My prayer is that he will see a great harvest of souls as a result of his dad's obedience to Jesus!

Since then, we have been partnering with other ministries to reach people in Pakistan and other nations with the Gospel. In one case, a man who was a terrorist received a Bible in his native language. He read the Bible, repented of his sins, and put his faith and trust in Jesus as his Lord and Savior. Since then, he has given out over 600 New Testaments to other terrorists, even though many Muslims are calling for his death!

I sometimes hear Christians in America say that we should wipe out the Muslims. I am grieved when I hear these words. Jesus died for them, just as He died for you and me. We need to pray for them and for those who labor to get the Gospel to them. I have met many Muslims over the years who are wonderful people. Unfortunately, they have been deceived, just as we all were before we made the decision to accept Jesus as our Savior.

I'm praying that God will break all fear in me, and that I will see them with God's eyes and heart. They are no different than you and me. They're just lost, and we have a responsibility to reach them with the Gospel of Jesus Christ. We're committed to reach as many Muslims as we can. Although my heart longs to be with Jesus in Heaven, there are many here on Earth who have yet to hear the Gospel.

# Chapter 21

# MIRACLES DO HAPPEN

"...Go into all the world and preach the gospel to all creation. Whoever believes and is baptized will be saved, but whoever does not believe will be condemned. And these signs will accompany those who believe: In my name they will drive out demons; they will speak in new tongues; they will pick up snakes with their hands; and when they drink deadly poison, it will not hurt them at all; they will place their hands on sick people, and they will get well" (Mark 16:15-18 NIV).

The following short summaries are just a few of the many times that we saw God move in miraculous ways. Considering all the times we have seen Him deliver us, you might think there would be an automatic expectancy, or even complacency, because He has always been so faithful to us.

But I can tell you, in that moment—with your life, your team's life, and His Word at risk—you don't take anything for granted. It's by faith you continue, and it's with every ounce of gratitude that you thank Him when you have left the Customs area safely—His Word and supplies in hand.

Once when I was in China, I had a team of ten Americans with a large load of Bibles for a tribal minority group—each person had two seventy-pound duffel bags filled with Bibles. All of our bags matched, so it was pretty obvious that we were traveling together.

We prayed as we always do before we cross any borders. We know God is the only One who can open the way before us. It definitely has nothing to do with us or the way we pack. I try to stay focused when I'm flying into a closed country because I never know who is watching, and I also want to be sensitive to the Holy Spirit's leading.

As we approached the Immigration hall, my stomach was the first place to feel the stress and pressure, but I knew not to let fear or anxiety in. So I prayed and immediately sensed the Holy Spirit's presence.

Recently, I've started praying that God would wake up people at home to have them pray for our border crossings. We are all in this together, so having more people pray is a blessing and I can definitely feel His presence.

After clearing Immigration, we walked over to the Customs area. I started loading bags onto carts to make it easier for the other team members to simply walk up to a cart and push it out the door. I remember noticing several Customs agents just walking around in the area. I breathed a quick prayer for God's supernatural deliverance. It has always been amazing to me to witness how opposed people are to God's Word, but then again, it makes sense because it's Truth.

When I turned to walk out of the room, there were four Customs guards lined up along the wall opposite of the X-ray machine. Ten people carrying 20 duffel bags—and we were literally going to have to walk out of that place by passing right between them and the machine. But as we passed through, the guards were totally oblivious to us. It was like we didn't exist. It was a miracle!

When we walked out, a Chinese lady named Rosie approached me and asked if I wanted a taxi. I replied, "No, I need a mini-bus!"

She asked how many were in my group, and when I said ten, she replied, "No, you need a van."

I said, "No, I need a mini-bus," but she insisted, "No, you need a van!"

Just then the other nine walked out with their bags and she said, "You need a mini-bus! You need a mini-bus!"

I hired her to take us to the hotel, and as we were loading the duffel bags, she asked, "Why do you have so many bags?" She also wanted to know why they were so heavy.

I said, "Americans—lots of souvenirs."

She smiled and said, "That works!"

A few days later, I contacted a tribal pastor to see if he would come to our hotel and pick up some of the Bibles. I found out through an interpreter that he couldn't afford the cost of a taxi, so I told him I would pay his fare. Two hours later, he showed up in a small van. We gave him more than enough money to cover the fare, and then loaded seven bags full of Bibles into the van.

He was thrilled. He kept saying, "God Bless You! God

Bless You!" as he shook my hand. I literally felt a blessing come upon me. He gave me the best gift he possibly could; I wanted to weep.

When I returned home, I shared this story with a friend, who told me they had been praying for us to be invisible. I told her, "Keep praying that prayer—it's working!"

-------------------------------------------------

On a trip to a city in China, I felt that the Lord wanted me to minister the Gospel using Chinese tracts. After crossing the border and dropping off my delivery of Bibles, I boarded a train for this city. I arrived after dark, so I checked into a hotel and committed the trip to the Lord. That night I handed out tracts all around the area where I was staying. When I went to bed, I put the remaining tracts on my outside window sill, in case the police searched my room.

The next day when I woke up, I looked out my window. Right across the street from my hotel was a huge police station! I looked around the city and prayed to know God's strategy.

Later, I started handing out tracts and people were very receptive. I found construction sites and handed them out there. I gave them to restaurant workers. At night, when people were out walking along the streets, it was a great opportunity to hand out more.

As I was walking back to the hotel, I saw some police

walking behind me. I quickly went to my room, where it seemed like the tracts were multiplying—there were definitely more of them than when I started! Once again, I put them outside the window.

The following morning, I decided to bring the tracts inside. I put them in the bottom of my backpack, under my clothes. I could hear voices outside my window, so I opened the curtain. Two Chinese women from upstairs were trying to reach something on the roof outside my window; they were using a bamboo pole.

A few minutes later, I heard a knock at the door. Two Chinese men wearing suits and the two Chinese ladies, who were wearing skirts, walked past me into my room. The ladies opened the window; one of them climbed up on the desk and stepped out of the window. The two men stayed and looked around my room. They were all talking in Chinese. Before long, the lady on the roof climbed back in with a skirt in her hand. They thanked me and walked out the door.

I was getting ready to take a shower when I saw the skirt lying on the desk. Worried that it was a ploy for them to get back into my room and search through my belongings, I picked up the skirt and carried it out to the hallway. I found the four people, who looked very surprised when I handed them back the skirt. Immediately, I returned to my room, packed up all my stuff, and left the city.

When I returned to the States and shared this story, a friend asked me when this had happened. They had a dream at that very time, and in the dream, I was about to get arrested. The Lord told them to get up and pray so I wouldn't get arrested. I'm thankful for obedient prayer warriors!

-----------------------------------------------

On another trip, three of us had crossed the border from Hong Kong into China with a big load of Bibles. We flew from southern China to Northwest China, where I used to live. We had thirteen bags with us; twelve of them were smaller bags, but each bag contained about forty to fifty Bibles. The last bag was a large, hard-sided suitcase and it was also full of Bibles.

In total, we had about 800 pounds of Bibles, for which we were charged $600.00 in excess baggage fees. However, we felt the cost was worth it, even if we only led one person to faith in Jesus Christ.

The bags had to be X-rayed for security purposes, so we called on God to help us. We didn't want the people who worked in security to be able to see the Bibles.

We boarded the plane and flew four hours to our destination. After we landed, we walked from the plane into the airport and began taking our bags off the luggage carousel. A friend met us and helped us load most of the bags into a taxi, but we discovered that three of the bags hadn't arrived, including the big one.

We explained the situation to a lady who worked for the airline. She told us that we should wait as they were probably coming on the next flight. She went on to suggest that maybe the big suitcase had broken open and that was why it hadn't made it. This was the last thing we wanted to hear! Once again, we immediately went to prayer, asking for the Lord's intervention.

We decided that our contact and I should get the Bibles we did have out of the terminal quickly. We left the other guy we were traveling with to wait at the airport to see if the missing bags were on the next flight. We loaded our eleven bags into a taxi and took them to the college where my friend lived. This is where they could be distributed to other contacts. To avoid attracting attention to ourselves, or being questioned by the security guard at the front door, we had the taxi driver drop us off near the back gate. We thought it would be best to bring the bags through the building's rear entrance.

The college is adjacent to a coal yard, which we had to cross to reach the school property. My friend and I had the use of two carts, which we put the four duffel bags onto, and we carried the other three bags on our shoulders. Loaded down with Bibles and pulling the heavy carts across gravel, we walked through the coal yard. Often the bags would slip off my shoulders, and the carts would tip over from time-to-time. Those two blocks felt like ten miles!

We prayed that we would get the Bibles through with no problem. However, when we arrived at the back gate of the school, we found it was locked. It was now about five o'clock in the evening, so it was still light. If it had been dark, we would have climbed over the gate and passed the bags over. But, in broad daylight, that would have been too obvious, so we had no option but to walk around to the front door.

While we were walking along the side street, a jeep drove towards us with a military leader and three other officers in it. We exchanged greetings, and thankfully, they continued past us. We were praying that they would not stop and question us about the number of bags or attempt to look at their contents.

This is part of the suspense that causes one's stomach to ache—knowing you could be arrested on the spot. Again, the Lord covered us and they drove on by, waving at us. We were so relieved! We entered through the front gate and then through the front door. Now, there was the security guard to deal with, but he just looked up at us and then went back to reading his book.

Both of us were worn out from hauling those heavy bags and pulling the carts. Thankfully, another contact came walking out and grabbed some of the bags. It was a welcome relief since we had to carry them up to my friend's apartment on the third floor. It also didn't look like there was as much luggage with the three of us sharing the load.

I was still concerned about the big suitcase being opened and wanted to go and find my friend. Our contact said we should wait and pray, so we did. He felt impressed to tell us not to worry, but to wait and meet up with our friend the next day.

The next morning we went to the hotel where we had agreed to meet, but our friend wasn't there. The hotel had no room for him, so he had gone to a different one. He thought I had been arrested, and I was concerned that he had been arrested. Thankfully, nobody had been arrested, and the big suitcase had not broken open. It came on a later flight, along with the other missing bags. Everything had made it through safely! We were able to give the Bibles to our contacts and they were very grateful.

# Chapter 22

# OTHER EXCITING EVENTS

"And truly Jesus did many other signs in the presence
of His disciples, which are not written in this book; but
these are written that you may believe that Jesus is the
Christ, the Son of God, and that believing you may have
life in His name" (John 20:30-31 NKJV)

Luther was the English name given to a Chinese man who
was particularly zealous in his witness for the Lord. He shared
Bible stories with his college roommates every night in their
dorm room, and although at first they resisted, it wasn't long
before they wouldn't go to bed until he told them another one
of his stories. One day, he told his professor of Communist
History about Jesus Christ. She later repented of her sins and
put her faith and trust in the Lord.

When Luther told the teacher who was discipling him
that he wanted to be baptized, I went to her apartment to take
part in his baptism. The bathtub was already filled with water
when I arrived, so I instructed Luther to change into a pair of
shorts and a t-shirt.

He closed the bathroom door behind him, and we waited.
After about ten minutes, we asked him if he was ready, and he
said, "No, not yet." We wondered what could be taking him so

long. We waited another ten minutes, but when we questioned him again, we got the same response. A few minutes later, I asked if I could come into the bathroom. Once I got in there, he told me, "I don't know how to baptize myself." He had never seen a baptism, so I had to explain how it was done, and that we would baptize him.

-------------------------------------------------------

At another Chinese brother's baptism, an older Christian brother was with the new convert while he was changing his clothes. When we opened the door, we saw water all over the floor. The older brother had already baptized the younger believer, while we were waiting.

-------------------------------------------------------

During the time, I was working as an English teacher in Northwest China, some of the other teachers and I decided to have a Christmas party for the Chinese Christians we were discipling. A lady who was the local newscaster for the whole province had been invited. We had a great time of praise and worship with the students, and then a good time of fellowship.

After the students left, we were able to share the Gospel with the newscaster. I felt led to talk about Christian marriages, which intrigued her since she had just found out that her husband had been unfaithful to her. We talked about the benefits of Christian couples praying together and how it strengthens a marriage. God truly prepared her heart to hear about salvation through Jesus Christ.

Two weeks later, the teacher who had invited the newscaster to the Christmas party, invited me over to her apartment for the newscaster's baptism. Since it was so difficult to find places to baptize Christians outside of the government church, it became our habit to use private bathtubs, which we did in this case. After her baptism, the lady was so touched by God that she was eager to tell everyone in her province about Jesus. She boldly shared the Gospel with even high-level government leaders.

---

When I lived in Northwest China, I worked with an underground church, which met in a building with mud walls and a red cross painted beside the doorway. It was a joy to fellowship with this precious family of believers. Their services were vibrant, and the people were bold in their faith. Due to the shortage of Bibles, the people memorized long passages of Scripture and shared them with each other, while testifying about what God was doing in their lives.

Attending this church was a faith-building experience for me—hearing how God answered their prayers and used them to share the Gospel. Friends would sometimes visit, making the trip from Hong Kong to bring Bibles and other discipleship materials for the underground church.

One of my friends was an evangelist from Australia.

He had taught himself how to read, write, and speak fluent Chinese by only using a book and a tape. He was asked to preach about the Holy Spirit at a service for the underground church. The meeting place was several miles out of town, so in order to get there we had to ride the bus. This meant we also had to switch buses at various stops. Along the way, we had to walk past a big army base. We didn't want the soldiers on guard to notice that we were Caucasians, so even though it was a hot day, we covered ourselves up. We just kept on walking and praying that we wouldn't be stopped.

We arrived safely at the church and my friend preached. Then the believers asked if we would pray for individual people. They brought a lady to me for prayer. She had been deaf in one ear for six years. As I prayed for her, I felt impressed by the Lord to move my finger in and out of her ear, and to say, "Be open, in the Name of Jesus."

After I prayed, she thanked me and walked away. A few minutes later, I saw her put her finger into her ear and then pull it out. She came back to me and said, "Thank you, thank you! Jesus just healed my ear. I was deaf in this ear for six years and Jesus has healed it—now I can hear!"

I wanted her to know that I am just an ordinary person. However, we serve an extraordinary God who desires to work through His people. He wants us to get to know the voice of the Holy Spirit, so that we can be obedient to Him and do what He wants in and through us.

# Chapter 23

# THE LIGHT WILL SHINE IN NORTH KOREA

"The people walking in darkness have seen a great light;
on those living in the land of the shadow of death a light
has dawned" (Isaiah 9:2 NIV).

North Korea has been on my heart for many years and I
have prayed for this isolated, oppressed nation. While more
information has surfaced about it in recent years, I have long
held a burden for its people with a desire to go firsthand.

Of all the places I've traveled, North Korea was one of the
most disturbing and oppressive. There's a spiritual climate of
imprisonment throughout; its citizens are bound and gagged

by fear, depression, and idolatry. We could feel this oppression as soon as we entered the country.

We traveled by bus from China, and then, crossed the Tumen River into North Korea. The Customs Hall in China was modern, orderly, and very convenient. We passed through quickly; then we loaded onto a minibus and drove about a block to cross the river into North Korea. The Immigration and Customs Hall was radically different on the North Korean side. This building was old and antiquated; the parking lot was only dirt, which was filled with large rivets that had been made by years of rain.

Upon arrival, we were ushered into a room where we met three guides that would serve as "chaperones" throughout our trip. We immediately had to show them our Bibles, cameras, and any Christian materials we had brought. They carefully inspected and counted everything before returning it to us. Then we proceeded to Immigration and Customs.

The process of entering North Korea was slow and exhaustive. The inspection and interrogation portion was the most intrusive I've experienced in over 30 years of travel. Our bags were thoroughly searched and then we were screened by three metal detectors. Finally, we were called, one-by-one, and given clearance to enter the country.

I was amazed at how beautiful the countryside was: very lush and green with many mountains and what appeared to be little villages that dotted the landscape. The houses were all sparsely furnished and constructed of white-washed adobe.

Occasionally, you could see a worker who was quietly tending to their fields.

Our guides informed us that we had to ask their permission before taking pictures and we were not allowed to photograph the local people. I didn't hear this and was quickly chided by one of them when I started to use my camera. In order to monitor this more closely, they kept our group outside of the populated areas. At the end of our trip, they checked our cameras and deleted any pictures they deemed unsuitable, or that did not portray their country in a favorable light. Photo censorship was just one of the areas they tightly controlled.

There also seemed to be an underlying fear censoring thought and expression. We asked one North Korean what her husband did for a living and if it was a good job. She immediately retorted that it was a very bad job, but the government said it was a good job; therefore, it was a good job.

It was surreal to see people on the streets going about their everyday life. Nobody smiled or greeted one another. They seemed to be in their own world, and it was sad to see the lack of interaction. As we drove through populated areas, we would smile and wave at people. At first they would act surprised, then some would look inquisitively and wave back; others looked away. It seemed they had been warned not to interact with foreigners, but you could sense they had a desire to know about the outside world.

The only place we saw people openly engaging with each

other was in the central market. I was surprised at the noise level; people appeared uninhibited. We were curious and interested to learn more. But once again, we were watched like hawks and chided several times when we wandered away from our group to seek out the real North Korea. Our guides tightly guarded us from any local contact, unless it had been prearranged for our tour.

Everywhere we traveled we saw murals and shrines honoring Kim Il Sung, founder of North Korea, and his son Kim Jong Il. Every North Korean household is required to have their pictures hanging on a wall and are forbidden to throw away their images from newspapers or magazines. They are also required to wear a lapel pin with their pictures on the left side above their heart and will get into trouble if they don't have it on.

Throughout the towns and villages we visited, we saw this worship of the "supreme leaders" displayed in other ways. It seemed to mock the God of the Bible and even Jesus Himself. At one school entrance, there was a mural of the supreme leader with little children all around him. I was reminded of how Jesus said, "Let the little children come to me."

While we were eating at several of the restaurants, they played a video which mimicked a church service. The people in the big hall sang worship songs to their leaders, led by attractive, Korean women who were playing musical instruments. The crescendo was a nuclear warhead headed to the United States, hitting America and destroying the country. The people rose to their feet in thunderous applause and resounding cheering, much like Christians would do at the return of Jesus Christ. When I realized the video was a mockery of a church service, I couldn't bring myself to watch it any longer.

We encountered similar worship services on the streets in one of the towns we visited. They had a set-up like a praise and worship band. We kept hearing the names of the leaders sung over and over again.

Among other anti-American propaganda, North Koreans are told that Americans eat their children, and South Koreans are all infected with AIDS, which is why they are not allowed to visit the North. We were praying outside a shrine when one of our guides became angry and asked, "Why do all Americans hate North Koreans?" This is what the government would have them believe, but I reassured her that many Christians in the United States love and pray for her people.

Government propaganda was present throughout our tour, which was carefully crafted to give the appearance of prosperity. We toured a fish packing plant housed in an attractive compound. It was a huge building with large pools for fish, but they were all empty. The place was meticulously clean and the outside garden tended, but there weren't any fish or employees. Even the meals put before us were meant to give the impression that there's an abundance of food, but the façade crumbled as we traveled off the main roads. There were big potholes in the streets, and it was run down. You could tell the people work very, very hard in the villages, but have a meager existence.

This importance of preserving their image is instilled early. We visited a school where the students were learning English and I had a good conversation with two young men who were about 13 or 14 years old. However, when one of them shared that his father was retired from the military because an injury had left him paralyzed, the other boy motioned for him not to speak about it. The impression was that they have a perfect society. To admit things aren't perfect was an admission that the leaders had failed.

We also witnessed a performance by a group of about fifty children aged 5 to 6 years old. While their performance was exceptional and the children were naturally gifted, when a little one made a mistake, we saw fear fall upon all their faces as they cringed. Afterwards, they were like robots when we talked with them. It was obvious they had been taught how to act around foreigners. Finally, I tickled two of the little boys and they started to laugh. Then, I saw real human beings.

I have never felt such intense spiritual warfare and it felt like I was constantly battling thoughts that it was not possible to bear any fruit. It would seem that I got victory over the battle in my mind, only to be fighting it again within ten minutes. I was thankful to have my Bible, to be able to pray continuously, and for our times of worship as a team.

The prevailing attitude throughout the country was that of hopelessness. Several times in prayer, I saw an old man bent over with a heavy burden weighing him down. Instead of receiving help from the government, they added more burdens to his back and further oppressed him. Psalm 34:18 says, "The Lord is close to the broken-hearted and saves those crushed in spirit."

There is a great need for prayer to break these strongholds over North Korea that control, torment, and imprison people. Only God can penetrate such a closed country! My heart cry is Isaiah 9:2, that all North Koreans will have the opportunity to see the truth and light of Christ. "The people walking in darkness have seen a great light; on those living in the land of the shadow of death a light has dawned." Christ alone can cause light to dawn in a land of the shadow of death. When His light shines, no one can extinguish it!

# Chapter 24

# HIS WORK CONTINUES

"Jesus came and spoke to them, saying, 'All authority has been given to Me in heaven and on earth. Go therefore and make disciples of all the nations, baptizing them in the name of the Father and of the Son and of the Holy Spirit, teaching them to observe all things that I have commanded you; and lo, I am with you always, even to the end of the age'" (Matthew 28:18-20 NKJV).

When I was a new Christian, I read this passage of Scripture and it hit me between the eyes. I realized that as a disciple of Jesus Christ, I had a personal responsibility to help fulfill the Great Commission. And this Great Commission wasn't just for home, but for the entire world.

With the Lord's grace, I was able to establish Asian Vision in 1994. After working with different ministries around the world, I sensed that God wanted me to start a ministry that would focus on getting His Holy Word into areas where people are hungry for the Truth of Jesus Christ. Years later, as a result of our expansion to Cuba, Romania, and Turkey, we changed the name of the ministry to Vision Beyond Borders.

As I traveled around the world, people would ask for Bibles in their own language. While we originally started out delivering Bibles, the ministry has grown. The intent of the ministry is to cross denominational lines and bring God's Church together to help persecuted Christians and reach out to the lost. We have sensed the need to not only provide the Scriptures, but to meet other needs as well.

Jesus said, ". . . for I was hungry and you gave Me food, I was thirsty and you gave Me drink; I was a stranger and you took Me in; I was naked and you clothed Me; I was sick and you visited Me; I was in prison and you came to me" (Matthew 25:35-36). This is what we want to devote ourselves to—ministering in the way He calls us to do it.

Our primary focus remains to get Bibles to those who want them in their own language. If people cannot read the Word of God, we have sought to provide it to them through hand-wind devices, so they can hear the Word in their own language. In many countries, we have provided videos and DVDs and have found Flannel Graphs to be a great tool to reach children around the world with the Gospel.

Over 20 years ago, we sent our first seed packages through the mail to Nepal. Our seed ministry has expanded so much that we have now sent over 40 million packs of seeds around the world to feed the hungry.

In Laos, the seed project helped poor villagers who would run out of rice after nine months, and then forage through the jungle trying to find roots or anything to sustain them. It is reported that kids are now growing bigger than their parents because of the increase in nutrient-rich vegetables in their diets. We praise the Lord, that through this project, parents now have a cash crop which allows them to buy basic medicines and send their kids to school.

We have also witnessed a decrease in opium production, while vegetable harvesting increases. This aids in reduced drug usage, which we pray will lead to better relational dynamics in families, especially for children and women, keeping them out of the sex trafficking industry.

As our teams travel, we see many children who are abandoned and orphaned. I'm grieved when I see street kids who are homeless and treated as throwaways by society. My prayer is that God will break into their lives and set them free from alcohol, drug addiction, and promiscuity. These kids are also at great risk of being trafficked. We feel called to provide aid to those who are offering a safe-haven for them. As a result, Vision for Children began with the goal of helping kids in orphanages (children's homes) get their physical needs met, receive an education, and learn the ways of the Lord.

The sponsorship program has grown and team members are able to visit the homes and minister to the kids regularly. Through this program we have also been able to help the Karen and Karennie refugees along the Burma-Thailand border. The Lord has enabled us to provide clothing, hygiene and medical supplies, emergency medical support, and a short-term medical clinic. It is a joy to see the Lord mend these broken children who have suffered so much.

The ministry has been actively involved in providing

quality new and used clothing for those in need around the world. We have distributed more than one million pounds of clothing. We have also been involved in numerous projects around the world to help meet medical needs and provide clean drinking water.

It has been evident in the work we do that the native missionaries are often best equipped to meet the needs of their people. They don't have a language and culture barrier, but often do not have the means to reach out to those from their own countries. Through the Vision for Pastors program, VBB supports the work of pastors and evangelists in persecuted countries with a small monthly gift. This allows them to concentrate on the work the Lord has given them to do in their country and to be more effective at reaching people in the Name of Jesus.

As we have witnessed followers of Jesus putting their lives on the line for the Gospel, we are not only challenged in our personal walk with Jesus, but also our level of service. We want to give our best in serving people and bringing them the help they desperately need. We seek to have a humble servant's heart for God's children, and as we do, God continues to open doors. We pray the Lord will keep our hearts softened and yielded to help us see the world as He does.

I believe if the Church in America focuses on what is important—loving Jesus with all of our hearts and obeying the Word of God—we can help fulfill the Great Commission together!

The mission of Vision Beyond Borders remains to help fulfill the Great Commission as stated by Jesus in Matthew 28:18-20, by meeting the spiritual and physical needs of all people groups from around the world.

From the very beginning, while I was still at CFNI, this Scripture was prophesied over me. It is what my life has been about. "By faith Abraham obeyed when he was called to go out to the place which he would receive as an inheritance. And he went out, not knowing where he was going. By faith he dwelt in the land of promise as in a foreign country, dwelling in tents with Isaac and Jacob, the heirs with him of the same promise; for he waited for the city which has foundations, whose builder and maker is God" (Hebrews 11:8-10).

It is *by faith alone* that I have obeyed the Master's voice to me. I went, not knowing, waiting on the Lord, watching Him make a way where only He could make it. In this, and in all things, the glory belongs to Him.

# END NOTES

Chapter 1

1. Lausanne Global Analysis, "Number of Christians in China and India," (Beijing: Lausanne Global Analysis, August 7, 2011), 4, http://conversation.lausanne.org/en/conversations/detail/11971#article_page_4

2. Todd M. Johnson, "World Christian Trends 2005," Presented at IFMA/EFMA in St. Louis, Center for the Study of Global Christianity, p. 3, http://www.gordonconwell.edu resources / documents/IFMA_World_Trends.pdf; Center for the Study of Global Christianity, "Christianity in its Global Context, 1970–2020: Society, Religion, and Mission," (South Hamilton: Center for the Study of Global Christianity, June 2013), 6, 15, http://www.gordonconwell.edu/resources/Global-Context-of-Christianity.cfm

3. Angela Lu, "Your Bible, Now Made In China," WORLD News Group, April 4, 2013, http://www.worldmag.com/2013/04/your_bible_now_made_in_china


Chapter 11

1. Joel C. Rosenburg,'s Blog, September 29, 2013, http://flashtrafficblog.wordpress .com/2013/09/29/an-historic-christian-awakening-is-under-way-in-iran-i-discuss-the-inside-story-in-this-20-minute-interview-with-dr-hormoz-shariat/; Joel Richardson,"Despite Persecution, Revival in Iran Continues!" WND, January 18, 2013, http://www.wnd.com/2013/01/despite-persecution-revival-in-iran-continues/


Chapter 14

1. U.S. Department of State, Trafficking in Persons Report, (Washington D.C.: U.S. Department of State, 2013), 7, http://www.state.gov/documents/organization/210737.pdf

2. "High Rates of HIV Infection Documented Among Young Nepalese Girls Sex-Trafficked to India," press release, July 31, 2007, http://archive.sph.harvard.edu/press-releases/2007-releases/press07312007.html

3. U.S. Department of State, Human Rights Report, (Washington D.C.: Bureau of Democracy, Human Rights, and Labor, 2009), http://www.state.gov/j/drl/rls/hrrpt/2009 /sca /136091.htm

4. U.S. Department of State, Trafficking in Persons Report, (Washington D.C.: U.S. Department of State, 2007), 23, http://www.state.gov/documents/organization/82902.pdf

5. U.S. Department of State, Trafficking in Persons Report, (Washington D.C.: U.S. Department of State, 2008), 7, http://www.state.gov/documents/organization/105501.pdf

Thank you for reading "By Faith Alone."
I hope it was an encouragement to you!

*To learn more about the work of VBB,*
*please visit the website:*

**www.VisionBeyondBorders.org**

*Online Book Orders:*

**www.byfaith-alone.com**

*Praise God for His Word going forth!*
*A portion of the proceeds from this book supports*
*Bible projects in closed countries.*